The Day after Domesday

The.holie.Bible.

conteynyng the olde
Testament and the newe.

Non me pudet Euangelij Christi.
Virtus enim Dei est ad salutem
Omni credenti Rom. 1.

The Day after Domesday
The Making of the Bishops' Bible

Jack P. Lewis

WIPF & STOCK · Eugene, Oregon

THE DAY AFTER DOMESDAY
The Making of the Bishops' Bible

Copyright © 2016 Jack P. Lewis. All rights reserved. Except for brief quotations in critical publications or reviews, no part of this book may be reproduced in any manner without prior written permission from the publisher. Write: Permissions, Wipf and Stock Publishers, 199 W. 8th Ave., Suite 3, Eugene, OR 97401.

Wipf & Stock
An Imprint of Wipf and Stock Publishers
199 W. 8th Ave., Suite 3
Eugene, OR 97401

www.wipfandstock.com

PAPERBACK ISBN: 978-1-4982-3343-9
HARDCOVER ISBN: 978-1-4982-3345-3

Manufactured in the U.S.A.

Illustrations in this book are from *The Holie Bible: Conteynyng the Olde Testament and the Newe* (London: R. Jugge, 1568), digitized by Princeton Theological Seminary Library, and from McKerrow and Ferguson, *Title-Page Borders* (Oxford: University Press, 1931).

Contents

List of Illustrations | vii
Preface | xi
Abbreviations | xiii
Introduction | xvii

1. "The Translation of the Bible . . . Committed to Mete Men" | 1
2. "Able Bishops and Other Learned Men" | 21
3. The Bible of the Largest Volume Commonly Read in the Churches | 56
4. "They Have Bought a Newe Bible" | 68
5. Influence of the Bishops' Bible | 77
6. Art in the Bishops' Bible | 91
7. "A New Translation . . . to Rectify the Former" | 114

Conclusion | 125
Appendix | 139
Bibliography | 143

List of Illustrations

Figure 1: Frontispiece to the 1568 Bishops' Bible, a portrait of Queen Elizabeth I, conjectured to be the work of Franciscus Hogenberg, with the royal coat of arms and the figures of Faith and Charity. | frontispiece

Figure 2: Prologue to the 1568 Bishops' Bible, the coat of arms of Thomas Cranmer, Archbishop of Canterbury (1532–34). | 6

Figure 3: Preface to the 1568 Bishops' Bible, the genealogy of Christ, with the coat of arms of Matthew Parker, Archbishop of Canterbury (1559–75). | 17

Figure 4: Initial letter "T," Neptune taming the sea horses, with initials "M.C.," at Exod 1:1 (1568). | 23

Figure 5: Title for the New Testament in the 1568 Bishops' Bible, royal coat of arms at the top and figures of Faith and Charity (McKerrow and Ferguson no. 129). | 30

Figure 6: 1 Sam 5, Philistines bring ark into house of Dagon, signed "VS" on right side below figure (1568). | 34

Figure 7: Initial letter "A," two women, one standing and one seated, at 1 Chr 1:1 (1568). | 36

List of Illustrations

Figure 8:   Title page to Apocrypha in the 1583 Bible, royal coat of arms at top between Justice and Mercy, lion and dragon at bottom left and right, "CB," initials of Christopher Barker, at center bottom (McKerrow and Ferguson no. 158). | 41

Figure 9:   Title to Apocrypha in Christopher Barker's 1584 Bible, arms of Elizabeth at top (McKerrow and Ferguson no. 168). | 43

Figure 10: Isa 1, the vision of Isaiah, coal of fire touching his mouth, signed "VS" in lower left (1568). | 45

Figure 11: The Evangelist Luke at the opening of his Gospel in the 1568 Bishops' Bible, with his symbol the ox, signed "VS" bottom right on wall just below ox. | 49

Figure 12: Rom 1, Apostle Paul seated at table, sword on floor (1568). | 51

Figure 13: Map, Journey of Paul, Acts 28 (1568). | 52

Figure 14: Title to Psalms in Christopher Barker's 1579 Bible, royal coat of arms at top, Memoria and Intelligentia at each side, "CB," initials of Christopher Barker, at either side, two cherubs at bottom supporting arms of Stationers Company (McKerrow and Ferguson no. 171). | 58

Figure 15: Exod 25, Ark of the Covenant, signed "VS" at bottom left (1568). | 62

Figure 16: Exod 29, Aaron as priest, signed "VS" at bottom left of priest and "SH" at bottom right of priest (1568). | 72

Figure 17: Map, the way of the people of Israel in the wilderness, Num 33 (1568). | 75

List of Illustrations

Figure 18: Gen 3, Adam and Eve in the garden with animals, serpent in the tree at center top, signed "SH" at the left lower third of picture (1568). | 80

Figure 19: Gen 7, Noah's ark in the flood, dove at the top descending with olive branch, signed "VS" at bottom left (1568). | 87

Figure 20: The Evangelist Matthew at the opening of his Gospel in the 1568 Bishops' Bible, with his symbol the angel, signed "SF" [?] on the chair where Matthew sits. | 88

Figure 21: Gen 1, the Garden of Eden with the Tetragrammaton on the sun, signed "SH" at the bottom left (1568). | 89

Figure 22: The Garden of Eden in Christopher Barker's 1583 folio edition (McKerrow and Ferguson no. 199). | 90

Figure 23: Title page to the second part of the 1568 Bishops' Bible, a portrait of Robert Dudley, Earl of Leicester, conjectured to be the work of Franciscus Hogenberg. | 92

Figure 24: Title to Psalms in Christopher Barker's 1584 Bible, royal coat of arms at center top, Fides and Humilitas at each side, ensigns of the four evangelists at the corners, crest of Sir Francis Walsingham center bottom (McKerrow and Ferguson no. 165). | 97

Figure 25: Judg 4, woodcut compartment, unfortunately printed upside down (1568). | 101

Figure 26: Exod 17:21, the tabernacle with the children of Israel camped about, signed "Cornelius" at lower left (1568). | 102

Figure 27: The Evangelist Mark at the opening of his Gospel in the 1568 Bishops' Bible, with his symbol the lion, signed "VS" bottom right. | 104

List of Illustrations

Figure 28: The Evangelist John at the opening of his Gospel in the 1568 Bishops' Bible, with his symbol the eagle. | 105

Figure 29: Initial letter "P," Daphne becoming a laurel tree, at 1 Cor 1:1 (1568). | 110

Figure 30: Initial letter "F," huntsman who shoots his daughter, at Eph 3:3 (1568). | 111

Figure 31: Verso to Ps 1 in the 1568 Bishops' Bible, the coat of arms of William Cecil, first Baron Burghley. | 112

Figure 32: Map, Holy Land and places mentioned in the four evangelists, verso to title page of New Testament (1568). | 115

Figure 33: Opening of the book of Psalms in the 1568 Bishops' Bible with a decorative "B" and a portrait of William Cecil, later Lord Burghley. | 117

Figure 34: Map, location of Garden of Eden, Gen 2 (1568). | 124

Figure 35: Note to Ps 45:9, referring to Christopher Columbus (1568). | 130

Figure 36: Woodcut border with pelican feeding her young, the printer's device of Richard Jugge, at center bottom, and at lower right a nightingale in a thorn bush with the word "ivgge" above (McKerrow and Ferguson no. 141) (1575). | 132

Figure 37: Title to New Testament in Christopher Barker's 1583 Bible, Tetragrammaton at top between two cherubs, hand holding a book with "verbvm dei manet in aeternv̄." "ER" at either side, "C.B." within center opening (McKerrow and Ferguson no. 203). | 133

Preface

MY INTEREST IN THE Early English Bible was kindled in a college undergraduate class that used Frederick G. Kenyon's *Our Bible and the Ancient Manuscripts* as its text. The Revised Standard Version was issued with considerable publicity in 1946. My dean, searching for classes for me to teach as a beginning teacher, handed me the book *The Ancestry of Our English Bible* by Ira M. Price and said, "The students are waiting. Go teach them!" That was the beginning of a love affair with the topic that continued even after retirement.

My research on the Bishops' Bible, the immediate predecessor of the King James Version, began in anticipation of the four-hundredth anniversary of the publication of the King James Version. A two-month summer grant in the late 1960s from the Folger Shakespeare Library in Washington, DC, and time in the Library of Congress gave me an acquaintance with the Bishops' Bible. That was followed by a visit to London and to the library of the British and Foreign Bible Society as well as to the British Museum. Numerous British churches still have memorials to the Bishops' Bible translators. A sabbatical from my school took me to the rare book section of the New York Public Library and to the library of Union Theological Seminary. It had one late printing of the New Testament and another listed in the catalogue, which it never had. I found some libraries with catalogue listings of the Bishops' Bible, but a look at Gen 3:20 with "britches" for Adam and Eve proved them to be a Geneva Bible.

Preface

A fellowship grant offering the opportunity for a year's study at the American Schools of Oriental Research in Jerusalem put this project on hold. My desire to complete this study was stirred by the year-long celebration of that four-hundredth anniversary of the King James Version. The story of the Bishops' Bible has yet to be adequately told.

My career in teaching and writing has included nearly fifty years of teaching a course in the History of the English Bible, the publications of *The English Bible from KJV to NIV: A History and Evaluation* and *Questions You've Asked about Bible Translations*, numerous published reviews of current English Bible translations, and countless lectureship series on the subject of Bible translation.

I hope that this work might kindle in others this same love of the study of the English Bible.

—Jack P. Lewis
June 11, 2015

Abbreviations

d.   died

DAB   *Dictionary of American Biography*

DD   Doctor of Divinity

DM   Thomas Herbert Darlow and Horace Frederick Moule. *Historical Catalogue of the Printed Editions of Holy Scripture in the Library of the British and Foreign Bible Society*. 2 vols. New York: Kraus, 1963.

DNB   *Dictionary of National Biography*

fol.   folio

HBD   *HarperCollins Bible Dictionary*

KJV   King James Version

LLD   Doctor of Laws

no.   number

RSV   Revised Standard Version

STC   *A Short-Title Catalogue of Books Printed in England, Scotland, and Ireland and of English Books Printed Abroad, 1475–1640*, compiled by Alfred William Pollard and Gilbert Richard Redgrave. London: Bibliographical Society, 1963 [1926].

Abbreviations

Scripture Abbreviations

Hebrew Bible/Old Testament

Gen	Genesis	Song	Song of Solomon
Exod	Exodus	Isa	Isaiah
Lev	Leviticus	Jer	Jeremiah
Num	Numbers	Lam	Lamentations
Deut	Deuteronomy	Ezek	Ezekiel
Josh	Joshua	Dan	Daniel
Judg	Judges	Hos	Hosea
Ruth	Ruth	Joel	Joel
1–2 Sam	1–2 Samuel	Amos	Amos
1–2 Kgs	1–2 Kings	Obad	Obadiah
1–2 Chr	1–2 Chronicles	Jonah	Jonah
Ezra	Ezra	Mic	Micah
Neh	Nehemiah	Nah	Nahum
Esth	Esther	Hab	Habakkuk
Job	Job	Zeph	Zephaniah
Ps/Pss	Psalm(s)	Hag	Haggai
Prov	Proverbs	Zech	Zechariah
Eccl	Ecclesiastes	Mal	Malachi

New Testament

Matt	Matthew	Phil	Philippians
Mark	Mark	Col	Colossians
Luke	Luke	1–2 Thess	1–2 Thessalonians
John	John		
Acts	Acts	1–2 Tim	1–2 Timothy
Rom	Romans	Titus	Titus
1–2 Cor	1–2 Corinthians	Phlm	Philemon
Gal	Galatians	Heb	Hebrews
Eph	Ephesians	Jas	James

1–2 Pet	1–2 Peter
1–2–3 John	1–2–3 John
Jude	Jude
Rev	Revelation

Apocrypha and Septuagint

Bar	Baruch
1–2 Esd	1–2 Esdras
Jdt	Judith
1–2–3 Macc	1–2–3 Maccabees
Sir	Sirach/Ecclesiasticus
Sus	Susanna
Tob	Tobit
Wis	Wisdom of Solomon

Introduction

FOR FOUR HUNDRED YEARS, the King James Version, first issued in 1611, has been the Bible for English-speaking peoples. Despite publicity accompanying the publication and sale of popular new versions, the King James remains "the Bible" for a majority of English readers; and the producers of more recent translations readily admit an indebtedness to it.

The King James Version, though issued in the early seventeenth century, is the culmination of religious, social, political, and literary strivings of sixteenth-century England. This century saw the English Church break away from the papacy and establish its own organization and doctrinal statements. The century produced the literary figures of Foxe, More, Spenser, Marlowe, Jonson, Bacon, and Shakespeare. It saw tension rise between the established church and those who would be more radical in reform.

Not a small factor in this intellectual foment was the movement to present the Scriptures to the English people in the vernacular. In the thirty-five years following 1535, the Bibles of Coverdale, Thomas Matthew, the Great Bible, the Geneva Bible, and the Bishops' Bible, as well as some lesser editions, appeared.

The studies of James Frederic Mozley have, within the past generation, furnished excellent treatments of the Bibles of Coverdale and Tyndale, and the studies of David Daiches and Charles Butterworth aid the student with the King James Version. No such aids are available for the Bishops' Bible. Though more than four hundred years have elapsed since the Bishops' Bible was first published in 1568, its story has never been adequately told. No book-length evaluation of it has ever been published. Students of the English Bible content themselves in treating it by repeating a few derogatory remarks borrowed from the old books. Very little independent study has been devoted to this Bible since Westcott's analysis of over one hundred years ago and since the British Society Catalogue was published at the beginning of the twentieth century.

A half-century ago, Edwin Eliott Willoughby, in a brief monograph of which only 250 copies were printed, devoted some attention to the relationship of the Bishops' Bible to the King James Version. Only three periodical articles dealing with the Bishops' Bible appeared in the twentieth century. English Bible handbooks devote only a few pages to it. For the study of this, the least known of the Tudor-period Bibles, there is not even an adequate bibliography available for guidance. This neglect is all the more surprising in view of the fact that Richmond Noble demonstrated quite convincingly that Shakespeare's earlier plays reflect his use of the Bishops' Bible and in view of the fact that the Bishops' Bible is the immediate predecessor of the King James Bible.

The Bishops' Bible, produced by Matthew Parker and his fellow bishops to offset the popularity of the Geneva Bible which contained notes objectionable to the church leaders, went through nineteen editions in the thirty-eight years (1568–1602) of its publication, time which spans a major portion of the reign of Elizabeth I and the first years of that of James I. The translators of the King James Version, in keeping with the king's instructions, used the 1602 edition of the Bishops' Bible as the basis for their revision of the English Bible.

Though it has been less thoroughly studied than the other significant versions, it is widely recognized that the Bishops' Bible had many defects, some of which were corrected in the 1572 printing. The Bishops' Bible greatly influenced church life in the Elizabethan period. Nineteen editions of the whole Bible were printed in the thirty-four-year period before 1602. The New Testament continued to be issued until 1633. Family records were still being kept in some copies one hundred years later.

Introduction

While making use of Westcott's earlier analysis, this study depicts briefly the religious, literary, and intellectual atmosphere that produced the Bishops' Bible. It further describes the place in the sixteenth-century translations filled by this edition, as well as reevaluates its contribution to the general study of the English Bible. This study investigates the history and qualifications of the men who were invited to participate in the translation project. It considers the method of procedure followed and gives attention to the distinctive features of the Bishops' Bible in its various editions. Attention is given to the notes, which were designed to correct the objectionable Calvinistic notes of the Geneva Bible, and to the artwork, which, though it changed from edition to edition, was the most elaborate of any found in first editions of the early English Bibles. Notice is taken of the criticisms Parker's project evoked and of the use made of the Bible in the Elizabethan church, culminating in the Bishops' Bible being revised to form the King James Version.

A suggestion from Cranmer's letter to Cromwell in which it is presumed that the bishops would not prepare a better Bible until "a day after domesday" gives the title to this study—*The Day after Domesday.*

1

"The Translation of the Bible . . . Committed to Mete Men"

THE REFORMATION WAS HALF a century old when the Bishops' Bible made its appearance. William Tyndale had been martyred thirty-two years earlier on October 6, 1536. Already the early Reformation leaders had departed the scene: Zwingli in 1531, Luther in 1546, Henry VIII in 1547, Melanchthon in 1560, and Calvin in 1564. John Knox lived on until 1572. On the continent, the reform had reached its zenith, and the ebb tide had set in under the impact of the counter-reformation. The third session of the Council of Trent to which England had refused to send representatives had concluded in December 1563.

England, however, after having vacillated between reform and Catholicism through the reigns of Henry VIII, Edward VI, and Mary Tudor, had ten years earlier with the accession of Elizabeth I (November 17, 1558) set itself to adopt the middle way along which the queen was so skillfully to steer the nation.

It is merely coincidental to the story of the Bishops' Bible that Mary Queen of Scots fled to England in May 1568, for it has not been established that the Bishops' Bible played any part in the Scottish Reformation or that it was widely read in Scotland. Equally coincidental is the fact that Miles Coverdale, who gave English its first complete English Bible and who prepared the Great Bible, would pass to his reward on January 20, 1569, five months after Matthew Parker sent the first copy of the Bishops' Bible to the queen. It mattered little that in slightly more than a year, in February of 1570, the papal decree of excommunication against Elizabeth would be issued.

At least of passing interest is the fact that the recusant seminary at Douay was founded by William Allen and Dr. Jean Vendeville on September 29, 1568, seven days after Parker announced the completion of his Bible, for from this region would come one of the attacks on Parker's production as well as the Rheims-Douay Bible.

English Bibles in this half century had gone forth thick and fast: Tyndale's New Testament in 1526, Coverdale's Bible in 1535, Matthew's in 1537, Taverner's in 1539, the Great Bible also in 1539, the same with Cranmer's preface added in 1540, and finally the Geneva Bible in 1560. Several had appeared in repeated printings. The Great Bible was printed in 1561, 1562, 1566, and 1568.[1]

England had already determined that the vernacular Bible should be accessible to all, for the injunctions of Elizabeth issued in 1559 contained the order to officials within three months to provide at the charges of the parish a copy of the "whole Bible of the largest volume in English" set up in some convenient place in each church so that "their parishioners may most commodiously resort unto the same, and read the same." Every person should read the book "with great humility and reverence, as the very lively word of God."[2] At visitations, inquiry was to be made whether any persons, vicars, or curates discouraged the reading of any part of the Bible in either Latin or English.[3] The chief issue remaining to be settled was that of who would supply a suitable Bible. During Edward's reign, seven editions of the Matthew's Bible, five of the Great Bible, and two of Coverdale's Bible had been printed. But at the time of the accession of Elizabeth (November 17, 1558), no Bibles had been printed in England since 1553, prior to the reign of Mary. While New Testaments and copies of Bibles were in portable sizes, of Bibles earlier printed in England, only the Great Bible portion containing Proverbs, Ecclesiastes, Song of Solomon, Wisdom, and

---

1. Herbert, *Historical Catalogue*, nos. 110, 117, 120, 122.
2. Gee and Hardy, *Documents Illustrative*, 421.
3. Foxe, *Acts and Monuments*, 552.

"The Translation of the Bible... Committed to Mete Men"

Ecclesiasticus published by Robert Redman in 1540 had been in convenient portable size.[4]

Though numerous editions of the New Testament had been printed during Edward's reign, how many of these Testaments and Bibles had survived Mary's searching in order to destroy them is unknown. To supply the need of Bibles for home and church, there were new printings of the Great Bible in 1561, 1562, 1566, and 1568. Abroad, the Geneva Bible, dedicated to Elizabeth, was issued in 1560 and 1562. Elizabeth granted to John Bodley the exclusive right to print the Geneva Bible for seven years;[5] however, the right was not exercised. Tyndale's New Testament was issued by Jugge in 1553, 1561, and 1566.[6]

As early as December 19, 1534, thirty-four years before the issuing of the Bishops' Bible, the upper house of convocation consisting of bishops, abbots, and priors of the province of Canterbury had petitioned the king to decree the making of a translation of Scripture:

> And that furthermore the king's majesty should think fit to decree that the holy scripture shall be translated into the vulgar English tongue by certain upright and learned men to be named by the said most illustrious king and be meted out and delivered to the people for their instruction.[7]

Nevertheless, Cranmer's efforts to stimulate the bishops into activity twice miscarried. When Cranmer had divided the New Testament out into nine or ten parts and sent them to the bishops and other learned men, "causing each part to be written at large in a paper book, and then to be sent to the best learned Bishops, and others, to the intent they should make a perfect correction thereof. And when they had done, he required them to send back

---

4. Herbert, *Historical Catalogue*, no. 57.
5. Pollard, *Records of the English Bible*, 284–85.
6. STC, 2872–73; Herbert, *Historical Catalogue*, nos. 104, 111, 121.
7. Pollard, *Records of the English Bible*, 177.

their parts, so corrected, unto him at Lambeth,"[8] Stephen Gardiner replied on June 10, 1535:

> I haue as gret cause as any man to desire rest and quiet for the helth of my body; whereunto I thought to haue entended and to absteyne from bookes and wryting, hauing finished the translation of Saynt Luke and Saynt John, wherein I have spent a gret labour.[9]

To this refusal and to Cranmer's surprise of it, a certain Mr. Thomas Lawney facetiously quipped:

> Your grace knoweth well (quod Lawney) that his portion ys a pece of Newe Testament, And than he being persuaded that Christe had bequeth hym nothing in his Testament, thoughte it were madnes to bestowe any labour or payne where no gayne was to be gotten, And besides this It ys the Actes of the Apostells, whiche were symple poore felowes, and therefore my lord of London disdayned to haue to do with any of their Actes.[10]

A second effort fared no better. On February 3, 1542, in reply to the archbishop's query whether the Bible could be retained "without scandal and error and open offence to Christ's faithful people," the bishops insisted that revision was essential. The New Testament was divided out into fifteen portions for perusal. Longland took Saint Mark; Gardiner, Saint Luke; Heath of Rochester, the Acts; Sampson of Chichester took Romans, and so on. Cranmer took Matthew, Goodrick of Ely took Saint John, and Barlow of Saint David's took the shorter letters of Paul.[11] In the fifth session (February 17), a Bible was presented containing passages out of the Old Testament marked by the clergy in various pages. The committee for examining the New Testament consisted of the bishops of Durham, Winchester, Hereford, Rochester, and Westminster, with Doctors Wotton, Day, Coren, Wilson, May, and

---

8. Strype, *Memorials of Cranmer*, 1:49.
9. Pollard, *Records of the English Bible*, 196–97, note 2.
10. Ibid., 197–98; cf. Mozley, *Coverdale and His Bibles*, 36–37.
11. Cited in Mozley, *Coverdale and His Bibles*, 272–73.

"The Translation of the Bible ... Committed to Mete Men"

others of the lower house of Convocation. The Old Testament was entrusted to the archbishop of York and to the bishop of Ely, with Redman, Taylor, Haynes, Robertson, Cox, etc., men skilled in Hebrew, Greek, Latin, and English.

However, Gardiner, the bishop of Winchester, at the sixth session (February 17) publicly read a list of one hundred Latin words in the Bible which he desired should be retained:

> Ecclesia, Poenitentia, Pontifex, Ancilla, Contritus, Olocausta, Justitia, Justificare Idiota, Elementa, Baptizare, Martyr, Adorare, Dignus, Sandalium, Simplex, Sapientia, Pietas, Presbyter, Lites, Servus, Opera, Sacrificium, Tetrarcha, Sacramentum, Simulachrum, Gloria, Conflictationes, Ceremonia, Mysterium, Religio, Spiritus Sanctus, Spiritus, Merces, Confiteor tibi Pater, Panis propositionis, Communio, Preseverare, Dilectus, Didragma, Hospitalitas, Episcopus, Gratia, Charitas, Tyrannus, Concupiscentia, Benedictio, Humilis, Humilitas, Scientia, Gentilis, Synagoga, Ejicere, Misericordia, Complacui, Increpare, Distribueretur, Orbis, Inculpatus, Senior, Apocalypsis, Satisfactio, Contentio, Conscientia, Peccatum, Peccator, Idolum, Prudentia, Prudenter, Cisera, Apostolus, Apostolatus, Egenus, Stater, Societas, Zizania, Christus, Conversari, Profiteor, Impositio manuum, Idololatria, Dominus, Sanctus, Confessio, Imitator, Pascha, Innumerabilis, Inenarrabilis, Infidelis, Paganus, Commilito, Virtutes, Parabola, Magnifico, Oriens, Subditus, Dominationes, Throni, Potestates Hostia.[12]

Under the weight of the demand, the whole effort ground to a halt. On March 10, Cranmer, at the ninth session, informed the upper house that it was the king's will that each testament "should be examined by both universities." Despite the protest of some bishops that "the universities were much decayed of late, wherein all things were carried by young men, whose judgments were not to be relied on, so that the learning of the land was chiefly in this convocation,"[13] the archbishop was determined to carry through

---

12. Pollard, *Records of the English Bible*, 274–75, note 2.
13. Strype, *Memorials of Cranmer*, 1:95.

with the pleasure of the king. There was no action in the universities, and nothing further was heard of revision.

Two days after the bishop's action, Anthony Marlar, haberdasher of London, received the sole right of printing the Bible for four years.[14] It indeed looked as though Cranmer's earlier prediction made to Cromwell on August 4, 1537, that the Bishops would not get around to a better revision until "a day after domesday" would be true.[15]

Bishop Hooper, from prison in 1554 in his *Appellatio ad Parlamentum*, urged the need of revision which he had discussed with learned men. Hooper insisted he could prove that the English Bible was nearer the Hebrew than the translation usually ascribed to Jerome.[16]

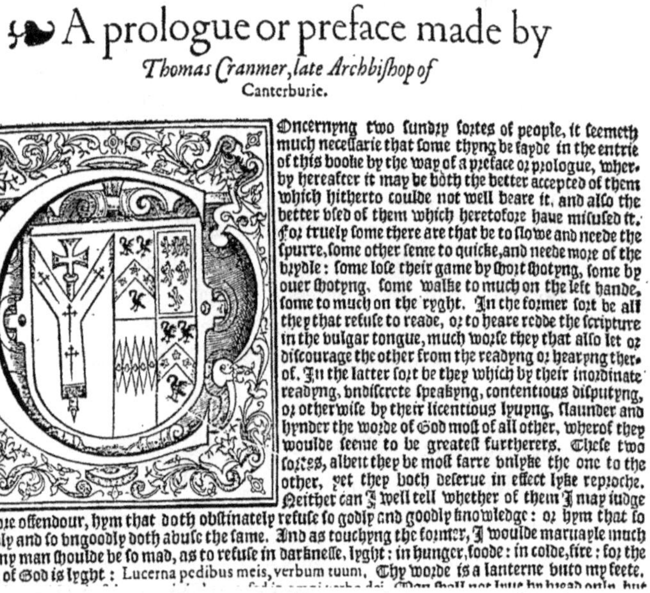
A prologue or preface made by *Thomas Cranmer, late Archbishop of* Canterburie.

C Oncernyng two sundry sortes of people, it seemeth much necessarie that some thyng be sayde in the entrie of this booke by the way of a preface or prologue, wherby hereafter it may be both the better accepted of them which hitherto coulde not well beare it, and also the better used of them which heretofore haue misused it. For truely some there are that be to slowe and neede the spurre, some other seme to quicke, and neede more of the brydle: some lose their game by short shotyng, some by ouer shotyng, some walke to much on the left hande, some to much on the ryght. In the former sort be all they that refuse to reade, or to heare redde the scripture in the vulgar tongue, much worse they that also let or discourage the other from the readyng or hearyng therof. In the latter sort be they which by their inordinate readyng, undiscrete speakyng, contentious disputyng, or otherwise by their licentious lyuyng, slaunder and hynder the worde of God most of all other, wherof they woulde seeme to be greatest furtherers. These two sortes, albeit they be most farre unlyke the one to the other, yet they both deserue in effect lyke reproche. Neither can I well tell whether of them I may iudge the more offendour, hym that doth obstinately refuse so godly and goodly knowledge: or hym that so ungodly and so ungoodly doth abuse the same. And as touchyng the former, I woulde marueyle much that any man shoulde be so mad, as to refuse in darknesse, lyght: in hunger, foode: in colde, fire: for the worde of God is lyght: Lucerna pedibus meis, verbum tuum. Thy worde is a lanterne unto my feete.

Figure 2: Prologue to 1568 Bible, coat of arms of Thomas Cranmer, Archbishop of Canterbury (1532–34).

14. Gairdner, *English Church*, 223–24.
15. Pollard, *Records of the English Bible*, 215.
16. Nevinson, *Later Writings of Bishop Hooper*, 393.

"The Translation of the Bible ... Committed to Mete Men"

But Cranmer's unexpected "day after domesday" finally arrived in 1568, thirty-one years later than Cranmer's revision effort, when on October 5, Matthew Parker, excusing himself because of illness, asked William Cecil to convey to Queen Elizabeth the finished product of his revision effort. An atmosphere that Cranmer could not have foreseen had developed which made the bishops anxious to act. Eight years before, the Geneva Bible had been issued by English refugees in Geneva and was making its influence felt in England. Parker described it as having "notis which might have ben also well spared."[17] The need of Bibles in the churches, the fear of the dangers of the use of diverse translations, and the undesirable features of the Geneva Bible all urged haste.

The Bishops' Bible first saw the light of day under Elizabeth; and though the New Testament was reprinted numerous times after her death, the entire Bible was never again reprinted after 1602, one year before her demise. This Bible is a phenomenon of the Elizabethan age.

The first hint that a translation project was in the wind was the letter of Richard Cox, bishop of Ely, to William Cecil, January 19, 1561.

> A nother thing ther is worthy to be consydered, the translation of the bible to be committed to mete men and to be vewed ouer and amended. I called apon it in bothe my masters tymes sed fustra. Yet god be praised, ye haue men hable to do it thoroughly. Thus muche I signifie to you because god hath apoynted you a speciall instrumente to the furtheraunce of his heavenly truthe, vnder so gratiouse a soverayn, who I trust doth not mislyke the apologie.[18]

From this suggestion, there seems to have been no immediate results. Cox further wrote Cecil in a letter received May 3, 1564:

> Syr I wryte to you the more seldom, because I contynew in consyderation of your weighty and Dayly affaires, and the importunitie of a numbre who let not to lade you with

---

17. Cf. Pollard, *Records of the English Bible*, 295.
18. Ibid., 287; Arber, *Transcript of the Registers*, 2:740.

letters, yet sumtyme I must trouble you beinge to me as I thanke god ye ar[e]. I wo[u]ld earnestly either by me selfes, or rather by you crave of the Quenes maiestie that she wolde Distribute emong the best learned of her clergye, the whole body of the *bible*, to be ouerseen and consydered, and the translation Diligently to be perused, to th[e] intent one vniforme translation might be vsed in all churches of her graces realme. A noble an acte as Ptolme Dyd by hys 7otie [*i.e., the seventy Jews who translated the Septuagint.*] The Diuersitie of translations make a fowle gerre [*gear*] in churches at this Day. Many good men are greved at it. And our Satans lawgh at it. And GOD nothing pleased with the colde handling of his cause. The whole *bible* may be Diuided in to partes, And such as shall be thought mete, to haue their portion appoynted to be Don[e]/agaynste a certayne tyme. At which tyme all the travailers to me[e]te together and to conferre as her highnes shall appoynte. Darke and Dowtfull places wo[u]lde be Declared as thei cum[e] in ordre with playne and breffe notes. Inkhorne and curiouse termes would be sho[w]ned playne and vsuall English sowght for. This was my request to our old masters of blessed memorye [*i.e. in the reigns of Henry VIII. and Edward VI.*] If our gratiouse mistres now would accomplish this godly acte, she would do GOD high seruice *et ego interim canos meos laetius ad miseros deducore.*[19]

About a century later, Thomas Ward pilloried England's reformation in Hudibrastic verse, in which he presented the whole as the result of official action:

> On this Account one master *Tyndal*
> Sets out his Bible; but Old *Gryndal*
> And other Elders two or three,
> Of *Naggs-head* Confraternity,
> Thought it not Right in every part,
> (Tho' *Tyndal* was a Man of Art)
> And therefore put in *Besses* Head
> To have another *Version* made.
> She grants, And Calls a *Convocation*

19. Arber, *Transcript of the Registers*, 2:741.

"The Translation of the Bible... Committed to Mete Men"

> Of the Choise Bishops of her Nation,
> Wherein, dissorder to Prevent,
> *Parker* himself sat President.
>
> ...
>
> And therefore why we are call'd hither,
> Is to adapt a New *Translation*
> To this New Faith we teach the Nation.
> Join all your Wits in one to do't,
> Mine shall not fail to help you out....[20]

But there is not the slightest evidence that any such gathering was actually held. Nor is there evidence that the queen was consulted or gave stimulus to the project. That idea was already rejected by Christopher Anderson[21] and John Lewis.[22]

At the beginning of her reign, the queen had coolly delayed the question of a translation:

> Queen Elizabeth on the morrow of her coronation (it being the custom to release prisoners at the inauguration of a prince)... one of her courtiers... besought her, with a loud voice, that now, this good time, there might be four or five more principal prisoners released; those were the four evangelists and the apostle St. Paul, who had been long shut up in an unknown tongue, as it were in prison; so as they could not converse with the common people. The queen answered very gravely, that it was best first to inquire of themselves whether they would be released or not.[23]

The next solid hint that something might be afoot is seen in the recommendation of Matthew Parker and Edmund Grindal to William Cecil on March 9, 1565, that John Bodley's privilege of printing the Geneva Bible be renewed:

---

20. Ward, *England's Reformation*, 283, 285.
21. Anderson, *Annals of the English Bible*, 394–95.
22. Lewis, *Complete History*, 238.
23. Bacon, *Moral and Historical Works*, 164; cf. Westcott, *General View of the History*, 96.

> Being enformed by this berer John Bodleygh that vppon his late sute to you for the renewing of his privilege with longer tearme, for the reimprintinge of the late Geneva Bible by him and his associates sett foorthe, you suspended to give your furderaunce vntill you had hearde owre advise. So it is that we thinke so well of the first impression, and reviewe of those whiche have sithens travailed therin, that we wishe it wold please you to be a meane that twelve yeres longer tearme maye be by speciall privilege graunted him, in consideracion of the charges by him and his associates in the first impression, and the reviewe sithens systeyned. For thoughe one other speciall bible for the churches be meant by vs to be set forthe as convenient tyme and leysor hereafter will permytte: yet shall it nothing hinder but rather do moche good to have diversitie of translacions and readinges. And if his licence, herafter to be made, goe simplye foorthe without proviso of our oversight as we thinke it maye so passe well ynought, yet shall we take suche ordre in writing withe the partie, that no impression shall passe but by owr direcion, consent, and advise. Thus ending we commende you to Allmightie god.[24]

Despite the generous spirit toward diverse translations expressed in this letter (quite different from that expressed earlier by Cox), Bodley does not seem to have succeeded in getting out an edition, for no Geneva Bibles were printed in England until after the death of Parker in 1575. Bodley's privilege of January 8, 1561, had contained the provisio:

> Prouided that the bible to be emprinted may be so ordered in the edicion thereof as may be seme expedient by the aduise of our trusty and welbeloued the bisshopps of Canterbory and London.[25]

In preparing his revision, Parker seems to have made assignments scattered over a period of time. On December 19, 1565,

---

24. Pollard, *Records of the English Bible*, 285–86; Bruce and Perowne, *Correspondence of Matthew Parker*, 261–62.

25. Pollard, *Records of the English Bible*, 285.

"The Translation of the Bible... Committed to Mete Men"

John Parkhurst, bishop of Norwich, wrote promising cooperation to the extent duties permitted: "I have received that part of the Bible appointed to me, and will travel therein with such diligence and expedition as conveniently I may."[26]

Edmund Guest, bishop of Rochester, returned his portion with a letter dated by the editor of the *Correspondence of Matthew Parker* as "probably 1565"; and while apologizing for the delay, affirming fidelity in the task and explaining his system of notation, he offers to do further work if it is needed:

> My duty humbly presupposed to your grace. These be to do the same to understand that, at the last, I have sent your grace your book again with such notes and advertisements that for my business I could well gather. I beseech your grace that when you have read them I might have them again, for Mr Secretary would see them. If your grace will have me to amend them I am at your commandment. I will be with your grace upon Friday to know your mind and to have the book. I have not altered the translation but where it giveth occasion of an error, as in the first Psalm at the beginning, I turn the preterperfect tense into the present tense, because the sense is too hard in the preterperfect tense. Where in the New Testament one piece of a Psalm is reported, I translate it in the Psalm according to the translation thereof in the New Testament, for the avoiding of the offence that may rise to the people upon diverse translations. Where two great letters be joined together, or where one great letter is twice put, it signifieth that both the sentences or the words be expounded together. Thus trusting that your grace will take in good part my rude handing of the Psalms, I most heartily bid the same well to fare in Christ.[27]

Meanwhile, progress reports drifted in from other workmen. On February 6, 1565, Edwin Sandys, bishop of Worcester, had finished his work and returned it with a letter:

---

26. Bruce and Perowne, *Correspondence of Matthew Parker*, 248.
27. Ibid., 250.

The Day after Domesday

> My duty remembered; According to your Grace's letter of instruction, I have perused the book you sent me, and with good diligence: having also, in conference with some other, considered of the same, in such sort, I trust, as your Grace will not mislike of. I have sent up with it my Clerk, whose hand I used in writing forth the corrections and marginal notes. When it shall please your Grace to set over the Book to be viewed by some one of your Chaplains, my said Clerk shall attend a day or two, to make it plain unto him, how my notes are to be placed.
>
> In mine opinion, your Grace shall do well to make the whole Bible to be diligently surveyed by some well learned, before it be put to print; and also to have skilful and diligent correctors at the printing of it, that it may be done in such perfection, that the adversaries can have no occasion to quarrel with it. Which thing will require a time. *Sed sat cito, si sat bene.* The setters forth of this our common translation followed Munster too much, who doubtless was a very negligent man in his doings, and often swerved very much from the Hebrew.
>
> Thus, trusting that your Grace will take in good part my trifles, wherein wanted no good will, I commend the same to the grace of Almighty God. From my house at Worcester.[28]

In yet another letter, Sandys urged haste:

> Your Grace . . . should much benefit the Church, in hastening forward the Bible which you have in hand: those that we have be not only false printed, but also give great offence to many, by reason of the depravity in reading.[29]

Two letters from Richard Davies, bishop of Saint David's, tell of his part. In the first, dated March 19, 1566, he acknowledges receiving his portion:

---

28. Pollard, *Records of the English Bible*, 288–89; Bruce and Perowne, *Correspondence of Matthew Parker*, 256–57.

29. Pollard, *Records of the English Bible*, 289; Strype, *Life and Acts of Matthew Parker*, 1:3:415–16.

"The Translation of the Bible ... Committed to Mete Men"

> Pleaseth it your grace to be advertised that I received that piece of the Bible which your grace hath committed to me to be recognized, the fourth day of March last; and your grace's letters dated the sixth of December, I received eight days before I received the portion of the Bible. I am in hand to perform your request, and will use as much diligence and speed as I can, having small help for that or for the Welsh Bible. Mr Salisbury only taketh pain with me.[30]

In the second letter, slightly more than a month later, April 24, 1566, he again wrote:

> I am well forward in the recognising of that part of the Bible that your grace hath committed unto me. I will by the help of God finish it with as much speed as I can. I bestow for the performance of the same all such time as I can spare from such affairs as will suffer no delays.[31]

Just a few days later, May 3, 1566, Richard Cox wrote:

> I trust your Grace is well forward with the Bible by this time. I perceive the greatest burden will lie upon your neck touching care and travail. I would wish that such usual words that we English people be acquainted with might still remain in their form and sound, so far forth as the Hebrew will well bear. Inkhorn terms to be avoided. The translation of the verbs in the Psalms to be used uniformly in one tense, &c. And if ye translate *bonitas* or *misericordia*, to use it likewise in all places of the Psalms, &c. God send this good travail a blessed success.[32]

On November 26, 1566, Parker announced to Cecil that the work is underway and invites him to participate:

> Sir I haue distributed the bible in partes to dyuerse men, I am desierus yf ye coud spare so moche leysur eyther in mornyng or evenyng: we had one epistle of S. Paul or peter, or Jamys of your pervsinge to thentent that ye

---

30. Bruce and Perowne, *Correspondence of Matthew Parker*, 265.
31. Ibid., 280.
32. Ibid., 282; Pollard, *Records of the English Bible*, 291.

13

> may be one of the buylders of this good worke in christes churche, although otherwise we account youe a common paterne to christes blessed word & religion, thus God kepe your honor in helthe.[33]

Nicholas Pocock suggests that this letter is wrongly dated and that it belongs to the year 1565, which, if true, makes it earlier than the preceding letters.[34] Cecil's reply has not been preserved, but the offer was probably a gesture of courtesy and as courteously declined.

We hear no more of the affair until the announcement of the completion of the project came on September 22, 1568. In a letter to Cecil, Parker wrote:

> Salutem in Christo. Sir I have receyved your lettres, and shall performe that yowe desier, concerning Mr. Welles when he cometh to me or any of his factors, I here his knowledge and honestye to be well reported. Sir, after much toyle of the Printer and sum Labors taken of sum parties for the setting owte and Recognising of the English bible, we be nowe come to a conclusion for the substance of the booke. Sum ornamentes of the same be yet lacking, prayeng your Honor to beare in pacience till yt be fuly reedy. I do meane by gods grace, yf my health will serve me better than yt is at this tyme, to present the Quenes highnes with the first, as sone as I can here her Maiestie to be come to Hampton Courte which we here will be within eight or nyne dayes. Which god prosper, and sent to your honor grace and health as I wishe to my selfe.[35]

However, the hoped-for improvement in health failed to come, and a few days later on October 5, Parker again wrote Cecil explaining a part of the procedure that had been followed and requesting that Cecil intervene with the queen to get a special privilege for the printer that he might not suffer financial loss should others "lurch him to steal from him these copies," and also

---

33. Pollard, *Records of the English Bible*, 287–88; Bruce and Perowne, *Correspondence of Matthew Parker*, 290; Arber, *Transcript of the Registers*, 2:741.

34. Pocock, "Bishops' Bible," 35.

35. Pollard, *Records of the English Bible*, 291–92; Bruce and Perowne, *Correspondence of Matthew Parker*, 333–34.

"The Translation of the Bible... Committed to Mete Men"

to seek to get a license from the queen for the use of the Bible in the churches.

> Sir after my right hartie Comendacions, I was in purpose to have offred to the Quenes highnes the first fruites of our Labors in the recognising the Bible, But I feale my health to be such, that as yet I dare not adventure. Whervppon for that I wold not have the Queens highnes and your honor to be long delayed, nor the poore printer after his great charges to be longer deferred, I have caused one booke to be bound as you see which I hartelye pray yow to present favorablie to the Queens Maiestie, with your frendlie excuse of my disabylitie, in not coming my self. I haue also wrytten to the Queens Maiestie, the Copie wherof I have sent yow the rather to vse your oportunitie of deliuerie, yf your Prudence shall not think them tolerable. And bicause I wold yow knewe all, I here send yow a note to signifie: who first traveiled in the diuerse bookes, though after them sum other perusing was had, the lettres of their names be partlie affixed in the ende of their bookes, Which I thought a polecie to showe them, to make them more diligent, as Awnswerable for their doinges. I have remembred yow of such observacions as my first lettres sent to them (by your advise) did signifie. Yt may be that in so long a worke things have scaped which may be Lawfull to euerie man cum bona venia to amend whan they find them non omnia possumus omnes. The Printer hath honestlie done his diligence, yf your honor wold obteine of the Queens highnes, that the edicion might be Licensed and only comended in publike reading in Churches, to drawe to one vniformitie, yt weare no greate cost to the most parishes and a Relief to him for his great charges susteined. The Psalters might remayn in Queres as they be much multiplied but wher of ther owne accord they wold vse this Translacion. Sir, I pray your honor be a meane that Jug only may have the preferment of this edicion, for yf any other shuld Lurche him to steale from his thes copies, he weare a great Loser in this first

doing, And Sir without doubt he hath well deserved to be preferred. A man wold not thinke that he had devoured so much payne as he hath susteined. Thus I wish your honor all grace vertue and helthe as to my self.[36]

Parker in his preface to the Old Testament gave as his reason for preparing the translation:

> And for that the copies thereof be so wasted, that very many churches do want their convenient Bibles, it was thought good to some well-disposed men to recognise the same Bible again into this form, as it is now come out, with some further diligence in the printing, and with some more light added partly in the translation, and partly in the order of the text, as not condemning the former translation, which was followed mostly of any other translation, excepting the original text, from which as little variance was made, as was thought meet to such as took pains therein.[37]

Near the end of Parker's account of his own life, he assigns the reasons for the printing: "that the old one was scarcely any longer to be met with, so many copies having apparently been destroyed."[38] Both Cox[39] and Guest[40] make clear that a fear of diversity of translations existed.

In his letter of October 5, 1568, which was intended to accompany the volume to be presented to the queen, Parker, without mentioning it specifically, suggested that the notes of the Geneva Bible had also made the new Bible desirable:

> For that in many Churches they want their Bookes, and have longe tyme loked for this: as for that in certaine places be publikely used sum Translations, which have

---

36. Pollard, *Records of the English Bible*, 292–94; Bruce and Perowne, *Correspondence of Matthew Parker*, 334–37; Arber, *Transcript of the Registers*, 2:742–43.

37. Reprinted in Strype, *Life and Acts of Matthew Parker*, 3:4:248–49.

38. Cited in Pocock, "Bishops' Bible," 35.

39. Arber, *Transcript of the Registers*, 2:741.

40. Bruce and Perowne, *Correspondence of Matthew Parker*, 250.

not been labored in your Realme; having inspersed diverse prejudiciall Notes, which might have ben also well spared.[41]

Already at this early period, the threat of Puritanism was being felt by the bishops. The Geneva Bible had gone through numerous printings.

Figure 3: Preface to 1568 Bible, genealogy of Christ, coat of arms of Matthew Parker, Archbishop of Canterbury (1559–75).

How much of the earlier cited revision procedure laid out by Cox in his letter to Cecil was followed, we cannot now determine.[42] That the revisers ever met and conferred together is unlikely. It is suggested by Guest's letter that Parker sent out Scripture portions—perhaps a dismembered Great Bible—upon which notations were made.[43] Both Sandys and Guest allude in their letters to

41. Ibid., 338; Pollard, *Records of the English Bible*, 295.

42. Arber, *Transcript of the Registers*, 2:741.

43. Bruce and Perowne, *Correspondence of Matthew Parker*, 250.

their systems of notation. Other knowledge of the procedure that had been followed must be pieced together from Strype's account and from Parker's address to the queen. Strype says:

> This our present Archbishop's thoughts ran much upon. And he had about this time distributed the Bible, divided into parts, to divers his learned fellow Bishops, and to some other Divines that were about him: who cheerfully undertook the work . . . The Archbishop took upon him the labour to contrive, and set the whole work a going in a proper method, by sorting out the whole Bible into parcels, as was said, and distributing those parcels to able Bishops, and other learned men to peruse and collate each the book or books allotted them; sending withal his instructions for the method they should observe; and they do add some short marginal notes, for the illustration or correction of the text. And all these portions of the Bible being finished, and sent back to the Archbishop, he was to add the last hand to them, and so to take care for printing and publishing the whole.[44]

To the queen, Parker explains:

> After my most Lowlie submission to your Maiestie, with my hartie reioyce of your prosperous progresse and retorne, pleaseth yt your highnes to accept in good parte, the endevor and diligence, of sum of vs your chapleins, my brethren the Bisshoppes, with other certaine Learned men, in this newe edicion, of the bible, I trust by comparisone of divers translacions put forth in your realme will apeare as well the workemanshippe of the printer, as the Circumspeccion of all such as have traveiled in the recognicion. Amonge divers observacions which have bin regarded in this recognition one was, not to make yt varye much from that translacion which was comonlye vsed by Publike order, except wher eyther the verytie of the hebrue & greke moved alteracion, or wher the text was by sum negligence mutilated from the originall. So that I trust your Loving subiectes shall se good cause in your Maiesties dayes to thanke god, and to reioyce, to

---

44. Strype, *Life and Acts of Matthew Parker*, 1:3:207–8.

see this his treasor of his holy worde, so set oute, as may be proved (So farforth as mortall mans knowledge can attaine to, or as farforth as god hath hitherto revealed) to be faithfully handeled in the vulgar tonge, besechinge your highnes, that yt may have your gracious favor, License and proteccion to be com[un]icated abrode, aswell for that in many Churches they want their bookes, and have longe tyme loked for this: as for that in certaine places be publikely vsed sum translations which have not byn Labored in your Realme having inspersed diverse preiudicall notis which might have ben also well spared. I have byn bolde in the forniture [i.e., prefatory matter] with fewe wordes to expresse the incomperable valewe of this Treasor amonge many thinges good profitable and bewtifull, ye have in possession, yet this only necessarie, whereof so to thinke, and so to beleve, maketh your Maiestie blessed, not only here in this your gouernance, but yt shall advance your maiestie to attaine at the last the blisse everlastinge, which after a longe prosperous raigne over vs, Almightie god send yow, as certainelie he will, for cherishinge that Juell which he loveth best, of which is pronounced that Quomodocumque Celum et terra transibunt verbum tamen domini manebit in eternum.[45]

To the queen, Parker, after giving the initials of the revisers, further explains the rules of procedure:

> Firste to followe the Commune Englishe Translacion vsed in the Churches and not to receed from yt but wher yt varieth manifestlye from the Hebrue or Greke originall.
>
> Item to vse such sections and devisions in the Textes as Pagnine in his Translacion vseth, & for the veritie of the Hebrue to followe the said Pagnine and Munster specially, And generally others learned in the tonges.
>
> Item to make no bitter notis vppon any text, or yet to set downe any determinacion in places of controversie.
>
> Item to note such Chapters and places as conteineth matter of Genealogies or other such places not edefieng,

---

45. Arber, *Transcript of the Registers*, 2:743–44; Pollard, *Records of the English Bible*, 294–95.

with some strike or note that the Reader may eschue them in his publike readinge.

Item that all such wordes as soundeth in the Olde Translacion to any offence of Lightnes or obscenitie be expressed with more convenient termes and phrases.

The printer hath bestowed his thickest Paper in the newe Testament bicause yt shalbe most occupied.[46]

The task had been gigantic; the outcome was impressive. And so highly pleased was this good prelate, when he saw an end put to this great work, that he seemed to be in the same spirit with old Simeon (Luke 2:29), using his very words, "Lord, now let thy servant depart in peace; for mine eyes have seen thy salvation."[47]

---

46. Pollard, *Records of the English Bible*, 297–98; Bruce and Perowne, *Correspondence of Matthew Parker*, 336; Arber, *Transcript of the Registers*, 2:744–45.

47. Strype, *Life and Acts of Matthew Parker*, 2:3:272; cf. *STC*, 1929a, fol. Ciir.

2

"Able Bishops and Other Learned Men"

FOLLOWING THE PROCEDURE OF Cranmer in his unsuccessful attempt at revision initiated in the convocation of 1542 and suggested by Cox in his letter to Cecil in 1561, Matthew Parker distributed the "parcels" of the Bible to others for revision. The workers cannot be definitely identified. Two lists of participants, unfortunately neither comprehensive, have been handed down. The first accompanies the letter sent by Parker to Cecil upon the occasion of the presentation of the completed Bible.[1] The second is compiled from the initials following some of the books in folio editions of the Bible. Parker explained that the names were "partlie" attached that the translators might be "more diligent as answerable for their doings." The initials are as follows:

>Deuteronomy—W.E.
>
>2 Samuel—R.M.
>
>2 Chronicles—E.W.
>
>Job—A.P.C.
>
>Psalms—T.B.
>
>Proverbs—A.P. C.[2]

1. Bruce and Perowne, *Correspondence of Matthew Parker*, 261–62; Pollard, *Records of the English Bible*, 335.

2. Strype, *Life and Acts of Matthew Parker*, 2:4:222, calls attention to the fact that the "C" stands separated in the print in this case, whereas it is joined at the end of Job.

21

The Day after Domesday

Song of Solomon—A.P.E.

Lamentations—R.W.

Daniel—T.C.L.

Malachi—E.L.

2 Maccabees—J.N.

Wisdom—W.C. (some copies)

Acts of Apostles—R.E.

1 Corinthians—G.G.

In addition, the initial letter of the 1568 edition of Genesis, Exodus, Matthew, Mark, 2 Corinthians, Galatians (some copies), Ephesians, Philippians, Colossians, 1 and 2 Thessalonians, 1 and 2 Timothy, Titus, Philemon, and Hebrews[3] has an "M.C." under it, which is thought to indicate its reviser.[4]

It would hardly have been thought necessary for the archbishop to affix his name at the end of his work to make him "more diligent and answerable" for his doings. Also, an "H.L." is attached to the initial letters of 1 Pet 5, 2 Pet 3, 1 John 5, 3 John, Jude, and Rev 22. It has been conjectured that this stands for Hugh Jones and that Jones took over work that in Parker's list is assigned to Bullingham.[5] The initials of William Barlow are only in some copies, and those of Edmond Scambler do not occur at all in the printed Bible.

The two lists chiefly correspond with each other as far as they go but diverge in that Parker's list is more extensive than the letters in the printed editions, and in that there is in Parker's list no mention made of an assignment of the Psalms and the section of the books from Ezra to Esther is not assigned to anyone.

---

3. Westcott, *General View of the History*, 100 note; Pollard, *Records of the English Bible*, 30-31.

4. Strype, *Life and Acts of Matthew Parker*, 2:4:221-22, and those who come after him, perhaps in error (certainly in ignoring Parker's list) assume that the entire Pentateuch was done by "W.E." Strype further assumes that the entire Gospels were assigned to Cox (Ibid., 2:4:222).

5. Westcott, *General View of the History*, 100, note.

1 **These are the names of the children of Israel, whiche came into Egypt with Jacob, euery mā came with his housholde:**
2 **Ruben, Simeon, Leui, and Juda:**
3 **Isachar, Zabulon, and Beniamin,**
4 **Dan and Nephthali, Gad & Aser.**
5 **All the soules that came out of the line of Jacob, were seuentie:**

Figure 4: Initial letter "T," Neptune taming the sea horses, initials "M.C.," at Exod 1:1 (1568).

Parker's correspondence elsewhere would suggest that Edmond Guest at first undertook Psalms. It has been conjectured, however, that Psalms was reworked by the person whose initials are "T.B." The identity remains conjectural with many supposing that it is Thomas Becon; but more recently, it has been suggested that Thomas Bickley is intended.[6] There is also the problem of "I Lich. and Covent.," the first letter of which seems to be a mistake for "T" and refers to Thomas Bentham, bishop of Lichfield and Coventry. Parker's list also suggests that Pearson worked on Leviticus and Numbers, thereby (with Parker's contribution) limiting "W.E." (Alley) to Deuteronomy rather than his revising the whole

---

6. Ibid., 99, note 3.

The Day after Domesday

Pentateuch as has often been asserted. On the other hand, Parker's list does not mention Hugh Jones.

From the archbishop's letter, one would conclude that at least fifteen assignments were made, to which must be added one for the Psalms where Parker's list is defective, another for Hugh Jones, and possibly another for the section Ezra to Esther where information is missing in both lists. Thereby, the participants must total eighteen and possibly nineteen names, one of whom is completely unknown.

The assignments seem to have been made over a period of time. Parkhurst acknowledged his assignment December 19, 1565; Sandys had finished his by February 6, 1565. Davies acknowledges his March 19, 1565, which seems to have been sent to him on the preceding December 6.[7] But it was not until November 26, 1566, that Parker invited Cecil to take "one epistle of S. Paul or peter or Jamys"[8] to revise. Pocock argues that the letter is misdated and should be considered as one year earlier,[9] and thereby it becomes one of the earliest portions of the assignment.

Cranmer's earlier revision project had stalled in the vain suggestion that the task be referred to the two universities, and King James later revived this procedure; but there is no evidence that there was a conscious effort on Parker's part to have equal representation from the two universities or to give prominence to the universities. The facts are, however, that of the men whose names have through the years been connected with the project, five are Oxford trained: Richard Davis, Thomas Bickley, John Parkhurst, Thomas Bentham, and Hugh Jones. Nine are Cambridge trained: Matthew Parker, Andrew Peerson, Edwin Sandys, Edmond Guest, Thomas Becon, Thomas Cole,[10] Edmond Grindal, Edmond Scambler,[11] and Gabriel Goodman. Six additional figures have connections with

---

7. Bruce and Perowne, *Correspondence of Matthew Parker*, 265.
8. Pollard, *Records of the English Bible*, 287–88.
9. Pocock, "Bishops' Bible," 35.
10. See note on Cole below.
11. Scambler later had a connection with Oxford.

both universities: William Alley, Andrew Perne, William Barlow,[12] Richard Horne, Richard Cox, and Nicholas Bullingham.[13]

The traits that the revisers had in common with each other have little to do with Bible revision. All have an impressive list of ecclesiastical services both before and after their joint project. Fourteen were bishops at the time of publication.[14] Bickley later became a bishop, while only Peerson, Goodman, and Perne never attained this rank. None of them lived to see their effort displaced by the 1611 Bible. Only Gabriel Goodman (d. 1601) lived until the beginning of the seventeenth century. If the earlier conjecture, now abandoned, that "T.B." refers to Thomas Becon were correct, he would have been the only one of the group whose death preceded publication of their work. Alley and Barlow did not live to see the third edition in which their work was considerably revised.[15]

As might be expected from the times, all revisers except Parker, Peerson, Alley, and Guest had been in exile during Mary's reign; but as Fuller puts it:

> Now the tidings of queen Elizabeth's peaceable coming to the crown was no sooner brought beyond the seas, but it filled the English exiles with unspeakable gladness, being instantly at home in their hearts, and not long after with their bodies.[16]

Several, no doubt, held views they had formed during the time of their exile. Parkhurst and Sandys opposed the requirement of old-fashioned vestments. Grindal also would go further

---

12. Barlow is claimed without evidence for Cambridge. See *DNB*, 3:233–34.

13. Bullingham received an LLD from Cambridge in 1559.

14. Parker, Alley, Davies, Sandys, Guest, Parkhurst, Barlow, Horne, Bentham, Grindal, Scambler, Cox, Jones, and Bullingham. Westcott's statement that there were eight bishops obviously is in error in view of the fact that in his note he proceeds to list nine (Westcott, *General View of the History*, 99 note 3). The statement also ignores Parker's list.

15. Thomas Cole (d. 1571) is now no longer thought to have been a participant.

16. Fuller, *Church History of Britain*, 4:261.

in reform than Parker or the queen.[17] Not only so, but in keeping with the trends of the times—for the clergy to marry—and despite Elizabeth's aversion to clerical marriage and despite the "Injunctions," all except Guest, Bickley, Perne, Grindal, and Goodman seem to have been family men.

More significant is the question of their linguistic equipment. Doubtless, the use of subordinates was employed in other cases than that of Sandys, who had used his clerk and suggests that Parker was doing the same. While a knowledge of Hebrew is to be assumed for all Old Testament revisers, it is specifically attested only for Alley, Grindal, Sandys, Guest, Horne, and Bentham. Grindal in his will made bequests of a Hebrew Bible and of New Testament and other books in Greek.[18] Even with these, the degree of mastery is in some cases a very questionable matter.

Perhaps the grasp of Greek in the New Testament group would come off somewhat better; however, Puritans in a statement not likely to be unbiased insisted "that their translation was patched together by men, 'few or none of them exactlie grounded in the sound and perfect knowledge of the Hebrew, Sirian, and Greeke tongues.'"[19] John R. Dore in the nineteenth century was of an entirely different opinion:

> But that the Bishops at both periods should be equal to such a task, one requiring biblical research, and accurate biblical scholarship, is a proof that in those days the sees were filled by Bishops of Rome, and afterwards by the Crown, not from favouritism, and political motives only, as has often been represented, but by men of the highest attainments.[20]

Strype insists that Parker "employed divers critics in the Hebrew and Greek languages to peruse the old translation, and to compare it diligently with the original text: and to compare likewise the Geneva translation, together with other translations

17. Knappen, *Tudor Puritanism*, 65–66, 176.
18. Nicholson, *Remains of Edmund Grindal*, 458–59.
19. Peel, *Seconde Parte of a Register*, 176.
20. Dore, *Old Bibles*, 238.

also."[21] As we will see, Strype is in error when he names Laurence as one who worked at this stage of revision.

Previous experience in Bible revision is also lacking for most of the participants. Parker and Grindal had petitioned Cecil on behalf of Bodley's printing privilege for the Geneva Bible. Davies and Goodman had worked on the Welsh Bible, the New Testament of which appeared one year before the Bishops' Bible. Cox had earlier served on a commission for making an authoritative version of the Bible and was at that time assigned to the Old Testament. His correspondence with Parker reflects a good grasp of the problems involved in Bible revision.

In the following survey, the initial given in the headings is that from the end of the various books where such occurs. The second item is from the list of Parker to Cecil, while the third item is the name of the figure involved or a conjecture to his identity.[22]

M.C.—M. Cant.—Matthew Parker

Matthew Parker (1504-75) was trained at Corpus Christi College, Cambridge, in which place he associated with a group—the "Cambridge Reformers." Parker's gifts of preaching led him to become chaplain to Anne Boleyn by March 30, 1535. By 1537, he had obtained his DD from Cambridge. Through the years, he served his college in various significant capacities as well as serving in church positions. Parker had married Margaret Halestone of Mattershall, Norfolk, June 24, 1547; and on an occasion of the termination of a visit of Elizabeth to Lambeth Palace, Elizabeth revealed her feelings on the matter of Parker's wife as she addressed her: "*Madam* I may not call you, and *Mistris* I am ashamed to call you, so I know not what to call you, but yet I do thanke you."[23] Parker had four sons, one of whom married the daughter of William Barlow, bishop of Chichester. He had one daughter.

21. Strype, *Life and Acts of Matthew Parker*, 2:4:223.

22. Earlier biographical accounts of the translators are to be found in Bagster's *Hexapla*; Pettigrew, *Bibliotheca Sussexiana*, 2:314-20.

23. Harington, *Nugae Antiquae*, 2:16.

The Day after Domesday

During the reign of Edward VI, Parker became dean of Lincoln (October 7, 1552); but following Edward's death, he supported Lady Jane Grey, which caused him to lose his positions. Though he remained in England during the time of Mary, he was in concealment and at times saved himself by flight in the night. "Flying in a night, for such as sought for me, to my peril, I fell off my horse so dangerously, that I shall never recover it."[24]

With the accession of Elizabeth, who had earlier by her mother been commended to his care, he was selected archbishop of Canterbury and was the second Protestant to hold this high position. He was chosen for the post despite Elizabeth's aversion to clerical marriages and was consecrated in Lambeth Palace on December 17, 1559, by William Barlow, John Scory, Miles Coverdale, and John Hodgkin. Parker's life is to an extent a story of the reform under Elizabeth. In 1562, the forty-two articles of the church were reduced to thirty-nine. He provided for a new edition of the Latin Prayer Book conciliatory to the Roman Catholic element. In 1565, he issued his "advertisements"; meanwhile at Cambridge, the Puritan party led by Thomas Cartwright made no little trouble for him.

Parker was renowned for his scholarship and left to the university library twenty-five manuscripts and twenty-five volumes. Beyond his work on the Bishops' Bible, Parker issued "The whole Psalter translated into English metre, which contayneth an hundredth and fifty psalms . . . Imprinted at London, by John Daye . . . Cum privilegio per decennium." It has been conjectured that 1567 is the proper date for this work.

There is also "The Gospels of the Fower Euangelists translated in the olde Saxons tyme out of Latine into the vulgar tongue of the Saxons. &c, London 4t. J. Daye 1571."[25] In this work, the Bishops' New Testament is printed along with the Anglo-Saxon. The dedication to Queen Elizabeth is by John Foxe.

Of the biblical books in the Bishops' Bible, Parker seems to have revised Genesis and Exodus from the Old Testament and Matthew, Mark, and 2 Corinthians through Hebrews from the

---

24. Bruce and Perowne, *Correspondence of Matthew Parker*, 59.
25. *STC*, 2961.

New Testament—at least Parker's own list so claims, and the initial under the opening letter of these books[26] would make it credible, thereby making Strype's suggestion, "The Archbishop's province was not so much to translate, as to order, direct, overlook, examine and prepare, and finish all,"[27] look very inaccurate. Parker seems to be the major contributor to the effort.

Parker died on May 17, 1575, at the age of seventy-one, and was buried in his private chapel at Lambeth. Though the original tomb was destroyed and his bones thrown out on the dung heap in 1648, Archbishop Sancroft later caused the monument to be restored. An oil portrait of Parker is at Corpus Christi College. Portraits are also in the university library at Trinity College, at Lambeth Palace, and in the guild hall at Norwich.[28]

Parker in his will, not forgetting his co-laborers, bequeathed remembrances to six of the participants in the revision: to Grindal there was a gold ring with a round sapphire; to Sandys, a staff of Indian cane with silver gilt at the end; to Horne, a gold ring with a turquoise setting; to Cox, a staff of Indian cane with a horologe on the top; to Bullingham, a white horse called "Hackengton" with the saddle, bridle, and a footcloth of velvet; and to Peerson, a silver cup with a cover gilt given to Parker by the queen on the feast of the circumcision.[29] Parker's copy of the first edition of the Bishops' Bible is listed in the catalogue of books presented to the library, Corpus Christi College, Cambridge.[30]

---

26. Galatians in some copies only; see Westcott, *General View of the History*, 100 note 3.

27. Strype, *Life and Acts of Matthew Parker*, 2:4:223; also Lewis, *Complete History*, 237.

28. DNB, 15:254–64; see also Strype, *Life and Acts of Matthew Parker*, 1:frontispiece.

29. Eadie, *English Bible*, 2:75.

30. Cotton, *Editions of the Bible*, 35; Strype, *Life and Acts of Matthew Parker*, 1:540.

Figure 5: Title for New Testament in 1568 Bible, royal coat of arms at top between Faith and Charity.

Parker's part in the revision, in addition to general supervision and the books he revised, included introductory matter:

The sum of the scripture

The Tables of Christes line

The argument of the scriptures
The first Preface into the whole Bible
The Preface into the psalter
The preface into the New Testament

A.P.C.—Cantuariae—Andrew Peerson [Pierson]

Andrew Peerson (or Pierson) was a graduate of Corpus Christi College, Cambridge, to which he had been admitted in 1541. Peerson earlier held minor posts; but he was made Parker's chaplain, almoner, and master of faculties when the latter became archbishop. At Parker's consecration, Peerson read the morning prayer.[31] Still later (1563), Peerson was made prebend of Canterbury cathedral. He was one of the executors of the will of Parker and received from him a legacy of a gilt cup. He was twice married and had one son. Peerson's death came on November 15, 1594.

Peerson revised the translation of Leviticus, Numbers,[32] Job, and Proverbs[33] for the Bishops' project. Tanner, according to Pollard, doubtfully ascribes to him Ezra, Nehemiah, Esther, Job, and Proverbs.[34]

W.E.—W. Exon.—William Alley

William Alley (1510–70), born at Wickham, Buckinghamshire, was educated at Eton and King's College, Cambridge,[35] with additional work at Oxford from which he received his DD on November 11, 1561. Alley, unrecognized as a priest, seems to have

---

31. Fuller, *Church History of Britain*, 4:287.

32. "A.P.C." is not found at the end of Leviticus and Numbers. That Peerson revised this section is conjectured from Parker's list.

33. Some copies of the 1568 edition do not have "A.P.C." after Proverbs. See Westcott, *General View of the History*, 100, note.

34. Tanner, *Bibliotheca Britannico-Hibernica*, 587, cited in Pollard, "Peerson or Pierson," 15:677.

35. Fuller, *Worthies of England*, 1:199.

spent Mary's reign in migrancy in the north country, in the role of physician and teacher. In Elizabeth's reign, he was elected bishop of Exeter on June 8, 1560, succeeding Miles Coverdale, who was not restored to his post after his exile; and Alley was consecrated on July 14 of that same year. Of Alley, it is said:

> He was verie well learned universallie, but his cheefe studie and profession was in divinitie, and in the tongs. ... the residue of his time, and free from his necessarie businesse, he spent in his private studies, and wrote sundrie bookes, whereof his prelections or lectures which he did reade in Paules, and his poore mans librarie he caused to be imprinted: the like he would have doone with his Hebrue grammar, and other his works, if he had lived.[36]

Alley was married and had one son. He died April 15, 1570, and was buried in the choir of his cathedral near the altar. His epitaph reads: "acerrimus Evangelicae veritatis Propugnator, morum probitate praecelebris, bonarum disciplinarum mirabili scientiâ clarus." He left behind among his works a manuscript for Hebrew grammar. His portion of the revision was the book of Deuteronomy.[37]

R.M.—R. Meneven—Richard Davies

Richard Davies was born in North Wales at an uncertain date. If he was eighty at his death, then he was born about 1501. If he was fifty when consecrated bishop,[38] then he was born about 1509. Davies was educated at New Inn Hall, Oxford. Under Mary, he fled with his wife to Frankfort and lived there, at least for a time, on alms, "bey dem Prediger closter."[39] There is no documentary evidence

---

36. *DNB*, 1:326.

37. The often met statement that Alley was assigned the entire Pentateuch ignores Parker's list. *DNB*, 1:326-27.

38. Strype, *Life and Acts of Matthew Parker*, 1:2:127.

39. Garrett, *Marian Exiles*, 54.

that he was ever in Geneva. At Frankfort, he was appealed to by John Hales to aid in quieting the strife in the church.

With Elizabeth's accession, he returned to England and was reinstated in his former positions. At first, he was appointed bishop of Saint Asaph; but in the spring of 1561, he was transferred to the bishopric of Saint David's. Much more prominent in Wales than in England, he became the adviser of Parker and Cecil in all Welsh affairs and corresponded with both officials. He sent to Cecil all of the ancient manuscripts and "monuments" connected with his see.

Davies was active in circulation of theological literature in Welsh and, in cooperation with William Salisbury, promoted the printing of the Welsh New Testament that appeared in 1567. Davies had translated 1 Timothy, Hebrews, James, 1 and 2 Peter, and had also contributed a long epistle to the Welsh for that Bible. The Welsh Old Testament did not appear until 1588, after Davies's death. Davies had three sons and two daughters.

In a letter to Parker dated March 19, 1565, Davies acknowledges receiving both a portion for revision and a letter from Parker requesting that he participate.[40] Later (April 24, 1566), he again writes, stating that he was devoting all the time he could spare and would finish as speedily as he could.[41]

In Parker's list, the books of Joshua, Judges, Ruth, and 1 and 2 Kings (possibly Samuel as well) were assigned to Davies. In the printed copy of the Bishops' Bible, his initials occur at the end of 2 Samuel. The last previous initial occurs after the end of Deuteronomy.[42] It is likely that Davies's work is limited to this group of books—Joshua to 2 Samuel—despite their lack of initials. These books closely follow the Great Bible, but there are ample evidences of unfortunate departures from it.

Davies died November 7, 1581, at the possible age of eighty and was buried in Abergwili Church of Saint David.[43] The original

---

40. Bruce and Perowne, *Correspondence of Matthew Parker*, 265.

41. Strype, *Life and Acts of Matthew Parker*, 1:3:416.

42. Webster's *Biographical Dictionary* is in error in attributing Deuteronomy to Davies. Neither list would support this assertion.

43. *DNB*, 5:599–602.

monument was broken in the restoration of 1883, and a substitute was provided. Also, the monument erected in 1888 in the cathedral yard of Saint Asaph in commemoration of the tercentenary of the publication of Bishop Morgan's Bible has a conventional representation of Davies. No picture of him is known.[44]

Figure 6: 1 Sam 5, Philistines bring ark into house of Dagon, "VS" on right side below figure (1568).

E.W.—Ed. Wigorn—Edwin Sandys

Edwin Sandys (1516[?]–88), born at Esthwaite Hall, Lancashire, was educated at Saint John's College, Cambridge, and rose to be vice chancellor of the university. A partisan of Northumberland, he was inclined to the claims of Lady Jane Grey; but with her fall, he proclaimed Queen Mary in the marketplace of Cambridge. On July 25, 1553, he was imprisoned in the Tower; but after thirty-eight weeks, he was released and, in company with Cox, Grindal,

---

44. Thomas, *Life and Work of Davies and Salesbury*, 36.

and Samson, sailed to the continent.[45] Garrett argues that Foxe has preserved Sandys's own account of his experiences as a fugitive and exile.[46] In turn, Sandys visited Antwerp, Augsburg, Strasbourg, Frankfort (Spring 1555), and Zurich. At Strasbourg, he lost his wife and child. At Frankfort, he was one of the committee for revision of the Prayer Book and, thereby, partly responsible for the Liturgy of Frankfort.

Sandys returned to England January 13, the day of Elizabeth's coronation.[47] He became bishop of Worcester on December 21, 1559. Though frequently engaged in quarrels, he nevertheless advanced in church positions. By 1570, he was bishop of London; and by 1577, he was bishop of York.

Sandys, while bishop, founded a grammar school at Hawkshead, Lancashire, which still preserves his Bible. Sandys was twice married and had seven sons and three daughters. One son, Sir Edwin Sandys, had close association with the early fortunes of the colony of Virginia and with those exiles who eventually settled at Plymouth in Massachusetts.[48] Sandys died July 10, 1588, two days before the Armada set sail, and was buried at Southwell Minster where there is an effigy in full vestments. Portraits are at Ombersley, Worcestershire, and at the Bishop of London's.

Sandys is characterized as being "a studious man and interested in the studies of others." Strype extols him as a man "well skilled in the original languages."[49] In a letter dated February 6, 1565, he makes known to Parker that he had consulted others, had used his clerk to write the corrections and notes he had made, and offers the aid of the same clerk when his work is to be revised by the chaplains of the archbishop. He further suggested that Parker have the whole project surveyed by some "well learned" before it was put in print as well as having correctors for the print. Despite the fact that Parker specified Münster as one of the versions to fol-

---

45. Foxe, *Acts and Monuments*, 8:590–91.
46. Garrett, *Marian Exiles*, 283.
47. Ibid., 283–84.
48. Ibid., 284.
49. Strype, *Life and Acts of Matthew Parker*, 1:3:415.

The Day after Domesday

low, Sandys criticized the translators of the Great Bible for having followed Sebastian Münster too much. He says Münster had "often swerved very much from the Hebrew."[50] Yet again, he urges haste in the project, insisting that the currently used Bible was "false printed" and gives offense "by reason of the Depravity in Reading."[51]

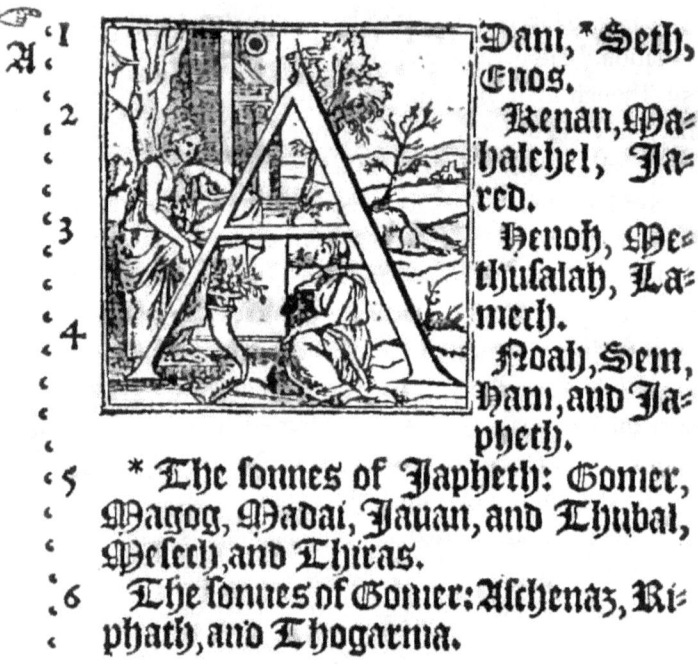

Figure 7: Initial letter "A," two women, one standing and one seated, at 1 Chr 1:1 (1568).

Sandys revised 3 and 4 Kings (1 and 2 Kings) and Chronicles. In the later edition of 1572, his share was the books of Hosea,

---

50. Ibid.; Pollard, *Records of the English Bible*, 288–89. Mombert, *English Versions of the Bible*, 267, insists that Sandys is in error and that Münster is literal to the extreme.

51. Pollard, *Records of the English Bible*, 289; Strype, *Life and Acts of Matthew Parker*, 1:3:415–16.

Joel, and Amos to Malachi.[52] An edition of his sermons is in the library of the Hawkshead School, which was founded by Sandys in 1584 or 1585.[53]

T.B.—(Missing)—Thomas Becon? Thomas Bickley?

The book of Psalms, as we have earlier seen, is unassigned in Parker's list. We know from a letter that it was first undertaken by Edmund Guest (1518–77). Guest, born at Northallerton, Yorkshire, was educated at King's College, Cambridge. He received his DD in 1571. Though on the Protestant side of disputations at Cambridge as early as June 1549, Guest remained in England through Mary's reign by a constant change of hiding places. He became chaplain to Parker in 1559. He participated in the revision of the liturgy. He was made archdeacon of Canterbury by Parker in October 1559, and then in turn installed Parker as archbishop on December 15, 1559.

Guest never married. He was elevated to bishop of Rochester, January 24, 1560. He aided in the drawing up of the thirty-nine articles of 1563 and claims to have penned the twenty-eighth article, which deals with the spiritual presence of the Lord in the Lord's Supper.[54] Guest was a favorite of Elizabeth and was elevated by her to the bishopric of Salisbury, December 5, 1571.

Guest died poor on February 28, 1577, at the age of about sixty-one, and was buried in the choir of Salisbury cathedral under a brass plate since removed to the northeast transept. He is represented in his effigy with his hair "short, moustachios on his lip." His literary productions include eleven items of letters, disputations, and treatises.

One of Guest's letters to Parker, with which he sent the part of the Bible that had been assigned to him, makes clear that he had worked on Psalms. In it, he states that he turned the preterperfect tense into the perfect tense in Psalm 1. He further succeeded in

---

52. Strype, *Life and Acts of Matthew Parker*, 2:222; *DNB*, 17:772–75.
53. *Remains Historical and Literary*, 143.
54. White, *Lives of the Elizabethan Bishops*, 129.

branding himself for all later generations as having followed one of the most asinine rules of translations in all the history of Bible production:

> Where in the New Testament one piece of a Psalm is reported, I translate it in the Psalms according to the translation thereof in the New Testament, for the avoiding of the offence that may rise to the people upon divers translations.[55]

Strype's conjecture that "R.E." at the end of Romans should be "E.R." (Edmundus Raffensis) and refer to Guest is unconvincing.[56] It is more likely that Romans was done by Cox.[57]

In the printed Bible, the initials "T.B." occur at the close of Psalms and are supposed by Strype to refer to Thomas Becon (1512-67). Educated at Saint John's College, Cambridge, Becon appears to have been extremely studious. Devoted to reformation principles, he was called upon in 1543 to recant his views. During the reign of Edward VI, he was chaplain to Cranmer and was made one of six preachers in Canterbury Cathedral. He was sent to the Tower on August 16, 1553, where he remained until March 24, 1554. He was deprived of his living and fled to Strasbourg, where he continued his literary work. Some time was spent at Frankfort where he lived in the Horse Market. He seems to have been a member of the Prayer Book committee in Frankfort, and he signed the letter to Calvin explaining that work.[58] Meanwhile, at home a proclamation of June 13, 1555, denounced the books of "Thomas Basil, otherwise called Thomas Becon." With the accession of Elizabeth, Becon returned to England in 1558. He was restored to his place and afterward received several other positions. Becon had five children. The total of his published works amounts to forty-seven titles.

---

55. Bruce and Perowne, *Correspondence of Matthew Parker*, 250.
56. Strype, *Life and Acts of Matthew Parker*, 2:4:223.
57. *DNB*, 8:759-61.
58. Garrett, *Marian Exiles*, 84-85.

Assuming that "T.B." is Becon, it is likely that the Psalms were assigned to Guest at first and perhaps were reworded later by Becon.[59]

A more recent conjecture on the identity of "T.B." is that he is Thomas Bickley (1518–96).[60] Bickley, born at Stow, Buckinghamshire, educated at Magdalen College, Oxford, and in 1553 became vice president of the college, served as chaplain at Windsor to Edward VI. During the reign of Mary, Bickley passed his exile in study at Paris and Orleans. Following the coronation of Elizabeth, he became chaplain to Parker, subscribed to the articles of 1562, and was rapidly promoted through several positions. He became chancellor in Lichfield Cathedral (1560), archdeacon of Stafford (1567), and warden of Merton College, Oxford (1569). He attained his bishopric at Chichester by 1585 in which position he served faithfully. Bickley's death came April 30, 1596, and he was buried in the cathedral. Though Fuller gives his age as ninety, the editor's note insists that seventy-eight is correct.[61] A tablet in his memory, attached to the north wall of Lady Chapel, shows him in a kneeling position. The Latin inscription states that he administered his diocese "piously and religiously, with sobriety and sincerity, the highest justice and singular prudence."[62]

A.P.E.—Cantabrigiae—Andrew Perne

The initials "A.P.E." attached to Ecclesiastes and the Song of Solomon are thought to be those of Andrew Perne (1519[?]–89), dean of Ely. Associated with Saint John's College, Cambridge, and later with Queen's College, he obtained his DD in 1552. He was incorporated at Oxford in 1553, and then was appointed master of Peterhouse in 1554. Perne was five times vice chancellor of the university. On December 22, 1557, he became dean of Ely. His

---

59. Ayre, *Early Works of Becon*; *DNB*, 2:92–94.
60. See Pollard, *Records of the English Bible*, 32.
61. Fuller, *Worthies of England*, 1:200.
62. *DNB*, 5:8–9; Garrett, *Marian Exiles*, 90.

religious history is characterized by numerous shifts of position (four times in twelve years), which included shifting to the new order of things when Elizabeth came to power. Perne is said to have had the finest private library in England in his time.

Perne died at Lambeth while on a visit there April 26, 1589, and he was buried in the parish church where a monument was erected to him. A portrait of him is at Peterhouse, Cambridge. Following his death, his fickleness became the point of satirists: "Old Andrew Turncoat," they called him, and a coat turned was said to be "Perned."[63]

J.N.—J. Norwic—John Parkhurst

John Parkhurst (1512[?]–75), translator of a section of the Apocrypha, was born at Guildford, Surrey, graduated at Merton College, and is reported by Wood as "better for poetry and oratory, than divinity."[64] Parkhurst was an advocate of reformation principles. In 1547, he had served as chaplain to Catherine Parr. In 1554, he went to the continent and was at Strasbourg by July 9. In October, he was active in Zurich where he lived with Rudolph Gaulter.[65] He was elected bishop of Norwich, April 13, and consecrated September 1, 1560. He was made DD at Oxford in 1566. Parkhurst was of Calvinistic leanings. There is evidence of considerable mismanagement of his diocese. He published a collection of Latin epigrams, some of which are eulogies or epitaphs on friends. His correspondence with the German reformers is preserved in the *Zurich Letters*. He was twice married but had no children.[66] When assigned his portion of the Bible, Parkhurst wrote to Parker (December 19, 1565) "that he would travail therein with such

---

63. *DNB*, 15:896–97; Fuller, *Worthies of England*, 2:464–65.
64. Wood, *Athenae Oxonienses*, 1:411–12.
65. Garrett, *Marian Exiles*, 244–45.
66. White, *Lives of the Elizabethan Bishops*, 152.

diligence and expedition as he might."[67] Parker's list assigns Ecclesiasticus, Susanna, Baruch, and Maccabees to Parkhurst.

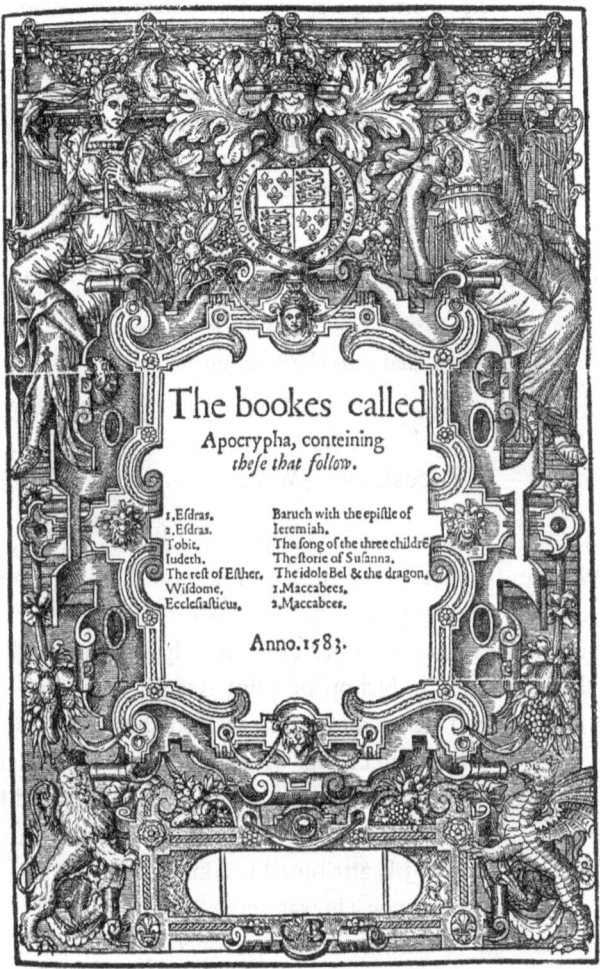

Figure 8: Title to Apocrypha in 1583 Bible, royal coat of arms at top between Justice and Mercy, "CB," initials of Christopher Barker, at bottom between lion and dragon.

67. Strype, *Life and Acts of Matthew Parker*, 1:3:416; Pollard, *Records of the English Bible*, 290.

The Day after Domesday

Parkhurst died February 2, 1575, at the age of sixty-three, and was buried in the nave of his cathedral at Norwich on the south side between the eighth and ninth pillars. The grave is marked by a monument.[68] The inscription as reported in Beloe and Wood reads:

> Johannes Parkhurstus, Theologiae Professor, Gylfordiae natus, Oxoniae educatus, temporibus Mariae Reginae pro Nitida conscientia tuenda Tigurinae vixit exul Voluntarius: Postea presul factus, sanctissime Hanc rexit Ecclesiam 16 annos, & mortuus est secondo die Februarii, an. 1574, aetatis suae 63.

There was also an inscription on one of three pillars of the cathedral:

> Viro bono, docto ac pio Johanni Parkhursto episcopo vigilantissimo, Georgius Gardiner posuit hoc.[69]

(Missing)—W. Cicestren.—William Barlow

William Barlow, translator for the books of Esdras, Judith, Tobit, and Wisdom (some copies omit the initial) is said to have become a doctor in the theological faculty at Oxford, but is also claimed without evidence as a member of Cambridge University. Barlow served successively as bishop of Saint Asaph (consecrated June 1536), Saint David's, Bath and Wells, and Chichester. His career is characterized by frequent change of religious position. Fuller calls him a man of "much *motion* and *promotion*."[70] He assisted in the making of "The Institution of a Christian Man" (1537).[71] An anti-Lutheran book of 1553 is attributed to him; but at the same time, he was a zealous reformer. He was active in ecclesiastical politics. During the reign of Mary, he was imprisoned in the Tower until he

---

68. *DNB*, 15:308–9; Fuller, *Worthies of England*, 3:209.

69. Beloe, *Anecdotes of Literature*, 2:58–59; Wood, *Athenae Oxonienses*, 1:413–14.

70. Fuller, *Worthies of England*, 3:249.

71. White, *Lives of the Elizabethan Bishops*, 5.

made a recantation. He then fled to Germany and served a congregation of English at Embden and then came to Poland.

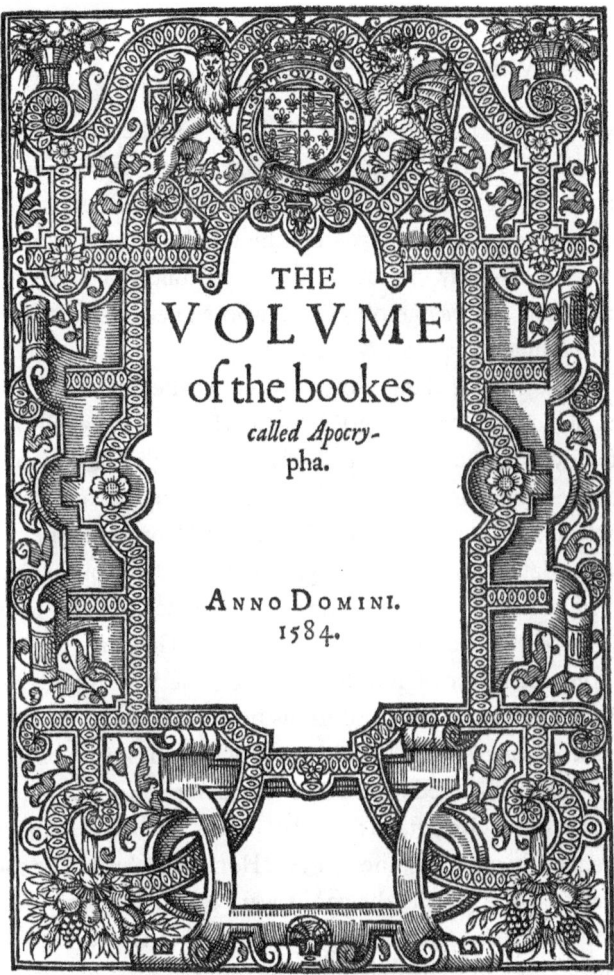

Figure 9: Title to Apocrypha in Christopher Barker's 1584 Bible, arms of Elizabeth at top.

Barlow assisted in the consecration of Matthew Parker (December 18, 1559) and was made bishop of Chichester. He had two sons and five daughters. One of his daughters was married to a son of Parker. He probably died December 10, 1569, and was buried at Chichester.[72]

R.W.—R. Winton—Robert Horne

Robert Horne (1519[?]–80), a native of Cumberland, was educated at Saint John's College, Cambridge, where he became senior bursar and Hebrew lecturer in 1545–46. Though DD at Cambridge in 1549, it was not until 1568 that he was incorporated as DD at Oxford. In his early church positions, he followed a program of reformation. He was among those who signed the forty-five articles of religion.

In the face of danger of being committed to the Tower by Mary, he fled to Zurich (April 5, 1554) via Strasbourg. Horne was invited by Cox to aid in the revision of the English liturgy in 1555 and signed the letter sent to Calvin. After expulsion of Knox from Frankfort, Horne was appointed reader in Hebrew for the church there and later pastor of the English congregation; but when new quarrels arose in the community, he ultimately moved to Strasbourg. It seems also that he was at Basel and Geneva.

The accession of Elizabeth opened the way for his return to England early in 1559 and to his position as dean of Durham. Later, he was elevated to the bishopric of Winchester, February 16, 1561. He administered his diocese with a harsh hand. Following a long term of service, after a period of illness, he died at Winchester House, Southwark, on June 1, 1580. Horne was buried in the cathedral near the pulpit. His goods were seized for debts owed to the crown. He had five daughters. A portrait at Trinity Hall, Cambridge, is thought to be that of Horne (but see letter of Bursar).[73]

---

72. *DNB*, 1:1149–51; Garrett, *Marian Exiles*, 89. Heaton, *Puritan Bible*, 230, confuses Barlow with a later figure by the same name who wrote an account of the Hampton Court Conference; see *DNB*, 1:1151–53.

73. Cooper and Cooper, *Athenae Cantabrigienses*, 411.

In the Bishops' Bible, the books of Isaiah, Jeremiah, and Lamentations were assigned to Horne. The initials "R.W." follow the book of Lamentations.[74]

Figure 10: Isa 1, vision of Isaiah, coal of fire touching his mouth, "VS" in lower left (1568).

T.C.L.—I. Lich. & Covent.—Thomas Bentham

Strype and Lewis assign these initials to Thomas Cole, Lincolnshire. Thomas Cole (1525–71) was educated at King's College, Cambridge, and spent Mary's reign at Frankfort where he served on the committee to draw up the new order. Garrett contends that the earlier effort to connect Cole with Geneva and the Geneva Bible is a result of confusing him with William Cole.[75] Back in England after 1559, he served as rector of High Ongar, Essex, and later at Stanford Rivers, Essex. Cole subscribed to the thirty-nine Articles

---

74. Garrett, *Marian Exiles*, 188–90; *DNB*, 9:1253–56; Fuller, *Worthies of England*, 158–59.

75. Garrett, *Marian Exiles*, 133–43.

in 1562 but is known to have a tendency toward nonconformity.[76] The effort of Lewis and Strype to connect Cole with Parker's project has been universally abandoned.[77]

Burnet has conjectured that a confusion of "I" and "T" has taken place to explain the discrepancy between the initials and the list of Parker.[78]

Thomas Bentham (1513–79), born at Sherburn, Yorkshire, appointed perpetual fellow of Magdalen College, Oxford, in 1546, was renowned for his scholarship. It is said that he,

> About that time did solely addict his mind to the study of theology and to the learning of the Hebrew tongue, in which last he was most excellent, as in those of Greek and Latin.[79]

Having distinguished himself for his reformation leanings under Edward VI, Bentham retired to Zurich in the days of Mary, April 1554. At Geneva in 1557, because of his knowledge of Hebrew, he was sought for collaboration in the Geneva Bible. He became a member of John Knox's congregation.[80] Eventually, Bentham came to preach while a student for exiles of Basel, until recalled to a congregation in London, despite the dangers attached to such a position. He was a member of the committee of light arbiters in the quarrel at Frankfort. It was he who stimulated the crowd in June 1558 to embrace the last of the martyrs burned at Smithfield during Mary's reign. Said Bentham, "We know they are the people of God, and therefore we cannot choose but wish well to them, and say, God strengthen them."[81]

Bentham was appointed bishop of Lichfield and Coventry, March 24, 1559–60, when he was forty-six years old. His death

---

76. *DNB*, 4:729–30.

77. Dore, *Old Bibles*, 238; Strype, *Life and Acts of Matthew Parker*, 2:4:222; Mombert, *English Versions of the Bible*, 269; Eadie, *English Bible*, 2:73.

78. *HBD*, 250.

79. *DNB*, 4:284.

80. Garrett, *Marian Exiles*, 86–87.

81. Foxe, *Acts and Monuments*, 8:559.

came twenty years later on February 21, 1579. His tomb at Eccleshall Church, Staffordshire, shows his effigy with his wife (Maude Fawcon of Hodley, Suffolk) and four children. There is the inscription: "Hic jacet in tumba Benthamus episcopus ille Doctor divinus largus patiens pius almus."

Bentham's share of the Bishops' project was Ezekiel and Daniel.[82]

E.L.—Ed. London—Edmund Grindal

Edmund Grindal (1519[?]–83), born at Hensingham in the parish of Saint Bees in Cumberland,[83] was educated at Magdalen College, Christ's College, and Pembroke Hall, Cambridge. He represented the Protestant side of disputations of June 24, 1549, and often thereafter. Ridley chose him as one of his chaplains in 1550, he later became chaplain to Edward VI, and he was one of the six to whom the forty-two articles were submitted for examination. At Edward's death, Grindal settled at Strasbourg from whence he wrote numerous letters to John Foxe.[84]

Grindal was at Frankfort in 1554 and later was a member of Cox's commission for Prayer Book revision and signed the letter to Calvin. He was also at Wesselheim and Speyer. With the accession of Elizabeth, Grindal was back in England on the day of coronation (January 15, 1559) and was selected as one of the preachers to explain the changes in the revised Prayer Book. When the Marian bishops were displaced, he was elected July 16, 1559, and consecrated December 21 of that year as bishop of London.

Grindal's sympathies lay with Calvinistic views rather than with the retention of the old forms of the past. In the midst of a bustle of activity, he was not of sufficient character to cope with the problems of his position. While personally conforming externally, he worked to save non-conformers from penalties.

---

82. *DNB*, 2:284; Fuller, *Worthies of England*, 3:410–11.
83. Nicholson, *Remains of Edmund Grindal*, i.
84. Ibid., 219–20.

The Day after Domesday

On April 11, 1570, Grindal was transferred to the archbishopric of York and then on January 10, 1576, to the archbishopric of Canterbury to succeed Parker. In this latter position, he proved too unbending to suit Elizabeth. After a running battle with the queen over "prophesyings" in which he was at first suspended from his functions for six months (1577), his death came in his house at Croyden on July 6, 1583. Grindal had remained unmarried and was buried in the parish church there on the south side of the altar.[85] The Latin tomb inscription is transcribed by Nicholson.[86] The memorial effigy was destroyed when Croyden church burned in 1867. The present church has a memorial tablet to Grindal, and a picture of him is at Lambeth Palace.[87]

Grindal had joined with Parker in 1565 in petitioning Cecil to renew Bodley's privilege of printing the Geneva Bible.[88] Grindal's portion of Parker's revision was the Minor Prophets. He bequeathed to the parish church of Saint Bees "my fairest English Bible, of the translation appointed to be read in the church."[89]

(Missing)—Ed. Peterb.—Edmond Scambler

Edmond Scambler (1510[?]-94), born at Gressingham, Lancashire, was educated at Peterhouse, Queen's, and Jesus Colleges at Cambridge. He preached the funeral of Jane Seymour. Scambler received his DD in 1564, and in 1584 he was incorporated at Oxford.

During Mary's reign, he ministered to a secret protestant congregation in London despite great danger. Under Elizabeth, he became chaplain to Parker; and on February 16, 1561, he was consecrated to be bishop of Peterborough. Later, on December 15, 1584, he was transferred to the bishopric of Norwich. Scambler was married to Julyan Fraunceyes on January 21, 1560[1], and had two

---

85. Strype, *History of Edmund Grindal*, 289; Fuller, *Church History of Britain*, 5:58, 59.

86. Nicholson, *Remains of Edmund Grindal*, xvi.

87. Brayley, *Topographical History of Surrey*, 3:316.

88. Pollard, *Records of the English Bible*, 285–86.

89. Nicholson, *Remains of Edmund Grindal*, 460; *DNB*, 8:704–7.

sons and two daughters. His death came on May 7, 1594. His tomb, formerly in Norwich Cathedral, was destroyed in the civil wars.

Scambler prepared Luke and John for the Bishops' Bible.[90] Earlier when vicar of Rye, Sussex, he had written *Medicine Proved for a Desperate Conscience.*

Figure 11: Evangelist Luke at opening of his Gospel in 1568 Bible, his symbol the ox, "VS" bottom right on wall just below ox.

R.E.—R. Eliensis—Richard Cox

Richard Cox (1500–1581), born at Whadalon, Buckinghamshire, was educated at Eton and at King's College, Cambridge, and at Oxford in which place he was imprisoned for circulation of Tyndale's New Testament. Cox became chaplain to Henry VIII, to Cranmer, and to Goodrick, bishop of Ely. He served on numerous commissions, including that which composed "The Necessary Doctrine

90. *DNB*, 17:885.

and Erudition of a Christian Man" (1540) and that which declared Henry's marriage to Anne of Cleves to be null and void. He was on the commission for making an authoritative version of the Bible and was assigned to the Old Testament.

Cox became royal tutor and advanced rapidly during the reign of Edward VI and aided in the making of the first Prayer Book (1549). From 1547 to 1552, he was chancellor of the University of Oxford.

But under Mary, Cox was suspected of being a part of Northumberland's plot and was deprived of his livings. On March 13, 1554, he had come to Frankfort and had led an English group in the use of Edward's Prayer Book. Here, his chief rival was John Knox, who led another group in a service on a Calvinistic model, until the expelling of the Knoxians brought peace to the region. While abroad, Cox also visited Strasbourg and Worms.

With the accession of Elizabeth, Cox became Bishop of Ely on July 28, 1559. After a service of twenty-one years, he was pensioned. His death came on July 22, 1581. His monument was defaced twenty years after his burial; but portraits are at King's College and at Trinity Hall, Cambridge. Cox was twice married, and he had three sons and two daughters, one of whom was married to the eldest son of Matthew Parker.

As early as January 19, 1561, Cox had proposed to Cecil that a revision of the Bible be undertaken:

> A nother thing ther is worthy to be consydered, the translation of the bible to be committed to mete men and to be vewed ouer and amended.... ye haue men hable to do it thoroughly.[91]

Later (May 3, 1566), when the work was doubtless well under way, Cox wrote to Parker:

> I would wish that such usual words as we English people be acquainted with might still remain in their form and sound, so far forth as the Hebrew will well bear; inkhorn terms to be avoided. The translation of the verbs in the

---

91. Pollard, *Records of the English Bible*, 287.

Psalms to be used uniformly in one tense, &c. And if ye translate *bonitas* or *misericordia*, to use it likewise in all places of the Psalms, &c.[92]

Figure 12: Rom 1, Apostle Paul seated at table, sword on floor (1568).

Cox translated Acts and the Epistle to the Romans for the Bishops' Bible.[93] With his opinions about uniformity in tense of verbs in the Psalms, above expressed, it is fortunate that he did not work on that book. Strype's conjecture that Romans was done by Edmund Guest (see above) is unconvincing. Robert Watt, doubtless in error, also assigns the four Gospels to Cox.[94]

---

92. Ibid., 291.

93. Garrett, *Marian Exiles*, 134–36; *DNB*, 4:1337–39; Fuller, *Worthies of England*, 38, 39.

94. Watt, *Bibliotheca Britannica*, 1:165u.

Ere haſt thou (gentle reader, for thy better inſtruction) the deſcription of the iourney and peregrination of Saint Paul, which is in this ſecond booke of Saint Luke called the Actes of the Apoſtles, moſt intreated of. And forbecauſe thou readeſt oftentymes of Emperours, Kynges, and Deputies, thou haſt ſet foorth to thee, the names, the yeres, and howe longe euery Emperour or Kyng raigned, or Deputie gouerned, and vnder whom any of theſe actes were done, euen vntyll the death of Saint Paul.

Figure 13: Map, Journey of Paul, Acts 28 (1568).

G.G.—D. Westmon.—Gabriel Goodman

Gabriel Goodman (1528–1601), born at Ruthin, Denbighshire, was educated at Christ's College, Jesus College, and at Saint John's College, Cambridge. After serving in several positions, Goodman was elected dean of Westminster, June 21, 1560. Though active repeatedly as a commissioner in ecclesiastical causes and though often nominated, he did not attain to a bishopric. Fuller says of him, "*Goodman* was his name, and *goodness* was in his nature."[95] His biography does not mention marriage.[96]

Goodman collected many rare books and manuscripts, chiefly Bibles, which were left to various colleges. In addition to his work on Corinthians for the Bishops' Bible, he gave both literary

---

95. Fuller, *Worthies of England*, 3:534.
96. Cf. Newcome, *Memoir of Gabriel Goodman*, 84.

and financial aid to the Welsh Bible endeavor, published in 1588, which aid is recognized in the preface of the publication.

Goodman's death came June 17, 1601. He was buried in Saint Benedict's chapel, Westminster Abbey, and a monument was erected on the south wall. A monument with a bust in a gown was erected in Saint Peter's Church, Ruthin, and a portrait is at the hospital.[97]

H.L.—(Missing)—Hugh Jones

Hugh Jones (1508–74) was educated at Oxford (probably New Inn Hall), and after serving in positions in Wales was elected to the bishopric of Llandaff on April 7, 1567, the first Welshman to hold the position for three hundred years. Jones was married and had several daughters. He died in poverty at Mathern in Monmouthsire, November 1574, and was buried within the church there.

It is conjectured that the "H.L." attached to the initial letters of 1 Pet 5, 2 Pet 3, 1 John 4, 3 John, Jude, and Rev 22 may be those of Jones and that he took up and carried to completion work previously assigned to the bishop of Lincoln.[98]

(Missing)—N. Lincoln—Nicholas Bullingham

Nicholas Bullingham (1512–76) was trained at All Souls, Oxford, and at Cambridge from which he received his LLD on January 10, 1559. His interests lay in civil and canon law, and he inclined toward reformed doctrines. Under Mary, he fled to Embden, December 5, 1554. With the accession of Elizabeth, he returned to his position as dean of Lincoln. He stood in for Parker at the confirmation and assisted in the consecration in the chapel of Lambeth House, December 17, 1559.

Bullingham was elevated to the bishopric of Lincoln, January 21, 1560. His knowledge of law brought him to serve on many

---

97. *DNB*, 8:130–31.
98. Ibid., 10:999.

important commissions for the settlements of the state and the church. On January 18, 1571, he was elected bishop of Worchester. He was a signer of the forty articles.

Bullingham was twice married and had children by both wives. While deeply in debt, he died April 18, 1576, and was buried in the Jesus Chapel on the north side of his cathedral at Worcester where there is an effigy. His epitaph reads:

Nicholaus Episcopus Wigorn

Here born, here bishop, buried here,
    A Bullyngham by name and stock,
A man twice married in God's fear,
    Chief pastor, late of Lyncolne flock,
Whom Oxford trained up in youth,
    Whom Cambridge doctor did create,
A painful preacher of the truth,
    Who changed this life for happy fate

18 April 1576.[99]

Bullingham had the Catholic Epistles ("canonical epistles") and the Apocalypse in the Bible project according to the list of Parker.[100]

Others—chaplains and clerks—doubtless worked on the revision.[101] A satirist said, "the chaplaynes trauiled, and the Bishopes brought forthe."[102] But since their contemporaries did not preserve their names, it is unlikely that we at this distance shall identify them. They, like the unknown soldier, must remain "Known only to God."

Numerous changes were made in various editions of the Bishops' Bible; but here again, none bothered to describe for posterity those to whom we owe this debt, whether to prelates, scholars, or merely printers. It seems that the latter are the most likely candidates in many cases.

    99. Ibid., 7:252.
    100. Ibid., 7:251–53; Garrett, *Marian Exiles*, 99.
    101. Strype, *Life and Acts of Matthew Parker*, 1:3:540.
    102. STC, 1929a, fol. Ciir.

We do know, thanks to Strype, of the influence of a certain Lawrence upon the 1572 and subsequent editions, which Lawrence has been conjectured to be Thomas Lawrence, headmaster of Shrewsbury School (1568-83). Strype describes Lawrence as of "great Fame for his Knowledge in the *Greek* Language, (and who read *Greek* to Lady Cecyl, afterwards Baronness Burghly, the Lord Treasurer's Lady)."[103] Strype lists Lawrence as one of the helpers in the original endeavor and supposed that his criticisms are directed toward earlier versions. But the facts seem to be that Lawrence is criticizing the first edition, to which he objects.

Westcott has argued that the traditional identification is untenable and suggests that the critic is Giles Lawrence (1539-84), who was Regis Professor of Greek at Oxford.[104] This Lawrence had been tutor of Sir Arthur Darcy's children during Mary's reign, later (1564) became archdeacon at Wiltshire, and still later (1580-81) archdeacon of Saint Albans. The date of his death is uncertain; but his successor became Regis Professor in 1585. His literary remains furnish no clear tie to the criticism of the Bishops' Bible.[105]

---

103. Strype, *Life and Acts of Matthew Parker*, 2:4:223.
104. Westcott, *General View of the History*, 237 note.
105. *DNB*, 11:697.

3

The Bible of the Largest Volume Commonly Read in the Churches

MATTHEW PARKER, IN HIS letter to William Cecil in which he requested that Cecil present the completed Bible to the queen, further requested:

> The Printer hath honestlie done his diligence, yf your honor wold obteine of the Queens highnes, that the edicion might be Licensed and only comended in publike reading in Churches, to drawe to one vniformitie, yt weare no greate cost to the most parishes and a Relief to him for his great charges susteined.[1]

To the queen, Parker further appealed:

> ... that yt may have your gracious favor, License and proteccion to be com[un]icated abrode, aswell for that in many Churches they want their bookes, and have longe tyme loked for this: as for that in certaine places be publikely vsed sum translations which have not byn Labored in your Realme having inspersed diverse preiudicall notis which might have ben also well spared.[2]

Unlike its predecessors, the Bishops' Bible carried no dedication to the queen. If, however, the queen ever publicly acknowledged Parker's labor, or gave it sanction, no record of such recognition has been preserved.

1. Pollard, *Records of the English Bible*, 293.
2. Ibid., 295.

The Largest Volume Commonly Read in the Churches

Efforts to see that the churches had Bibles were continuous. In the articles to be inquired of within the diocese of Canterbury for 1569, inquiry was made of the churchwardens: "Whether they had in their Parish Churches—the Bible in the largest Volume."[3] The articles are not to be interpreted as disqualifying the Great Bible from use, for it also could be called "the largest volume" as it had been in earlier decrees. The last edition of that Bible was issued in 1569 by Cawood and carried the words: "According to the translation that is appointed to be read in the Churches."[4]

With the passage of some time, Parker was, however, able to secure ecclesiastical authorization for his Bible. On April 3, 1571, the convocation of Canterbury ordered "every archbishop and bishop, every dean and chief residentiary, and every archdeacon should have at his house a copy of the holy Bible of the largest volume, as lately published at London [*amplissimo volumine, uti nuperrime Londini excusa sunt*[5]] and that it should be placed in the hall or large dining room, that it might be useful to their servants or to strangers," in cathedrals and in as far as possible (*si commode fieri possit*) in every church.[6] While the circulation of the Geneva Bible was not prohibited, it was printed abroad until after Parker's death in 1575, which factor no doubt reflects an effort to promote the Bishops' Bible in the churches. The Great Bible appeared in its last edition in 1569. Until the appearance of the Rheims-Douay Bible (New Testament in 1581, Old Testament in 1610, but not printed together until 1750), the Great Bible, the Geneva Bible, and the Bishops' Bible continued to vie for the English audience. The printer Jugge (and the assigns of Christopher Barker in the folio of 1578) used the words "set foorth by aucthoritie" to distinguish the Bishops' Bible.[7] The 1574 folio edition began to carry on the title page, "Set foorth by aucthoritie."

---

3. Lewis, *Complete History*, 257.
4. Herbert, *Historical Catalogue*, nos. 127, 128.
5. Cardwell, *Synodalia: Collection of Articles*, 1:115; Pollard, *Records of the English Bible*, 38.
6. Cardwell, *Synodalia: Collection of Articles*, 1:123.
7. Pollard, *Records of the English Bible*, 59.

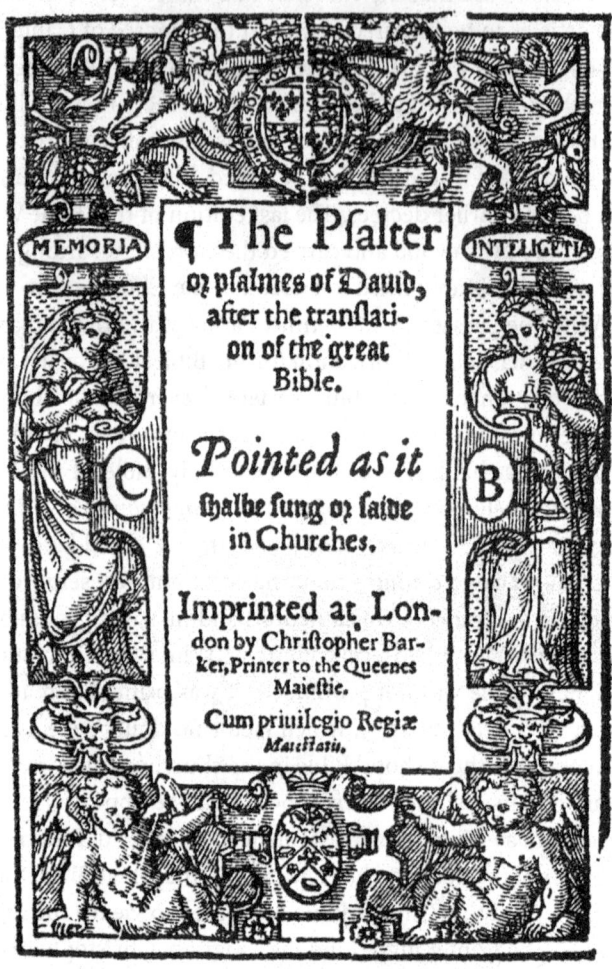

Figure 14: Title to Psalms in Christopher Barker's 1579 Bible, royal coat of arms at top, Memoria and Intelligentia at each side, "CB," initials of Christopher Barker, at either side, two cherubs at bottom supporting arms of Stationers Company.

The Scripture the clergy should read was not specified. The convocation at Westminster, 1575, ordered that:

> ... every parson, vicar, curate, and stipendiary priest, being under the degree of a master of arts, and being no preacher, shall provide and have of his own, within two months after warning is given to him or them, the New Testament, both in Latin and English, or Welsh; and shall confer daily one chapter of the same, the Latin and English or Welsh together.[8]

Uprisings like that in the north of the recusants, who tore up Bibles in the churches in Durham in 1569, described in letters to Bullinger both by Hillis and Grindal[9] normal wear and tear of use, and Puritan favoritism for the Geneva Bible created a need for further action by the authorities. Bishop Whitgift, as the first act of his episcopacy, acted to close up the gap and, after consultation with the bishops and with the assent of the queen, circulated on October 19, 1583, articles which ruled:

> That one kinde of Translation of the Bible be only used in publique service as well in churches as chapels and that to be the same which is now auctorized by the consent of the bishops.[10]

In 1583, number two in the articles offered by Whitgift to the queen read:

> That no book be printed unless allowed by the Archbishop of Canterbury and the Bishop of London; that no printer issue translations, editions, or annotations of the Scriptures other than those approved by the Bishops.[11]

In 1584, the phrase "authorized to be read in churches," and after 1588 the phrase "authorized and appointed to be read in churches," appeared on the title page of the Bishops' Bibles; but it was the authorization of the bishops and not of the crown. No

---

8. Cardwell, *Synodalia: Collection of Articles*, 1:137.

9. Robinson, *Zurich Letters*, 213–14, 218; Fuller, *Church History of Britain*, 4:16, 345.

10. Foster, C., *Lincoln Episcopal Records*, 147; Gee and Hardy, *Documents Illustrative*, 483.

11. Peel, *Seconde Parte of a Register*, 172.

royal proclamation, parallel to those of 1531, 1547, or 1559 for the Great Bible, was issued.

Whitgift wrote to Wickham, bishop of Lincoln, on July 16, 1587:

> Whereas I am credibly informed that divers, as well parish churches, as chapels of ease, are not sufficiently furnished with Bibles, but some have either none at all, or such as be torn and defaced, and yet not of the translation authorized by the synods of bishops: these are therefore to require you strictly in your visitations, or otherwise, to see that all and every the said churches and chapels in your diocese be provided of one Bible, or more, at your discretion, of the translation allowed as aforesaid . . . And for the performance thereof, I have caused her highness's printer to imprint two volumes of the said translation of the Bible aforesaid, a bigger and a less, the largest for such parishes as are of ability, and the lesser for chapels and very small parishes; both which are now extant and ready.[12]

It is thought likely that the folio and quarto editions of 1584 are the editions printed for this purpose.[13]

At the beginning of the reign of King James, convocation of the province of Canterbury assembled, March 20, 1603, and the eightieth canon was:

> If any parishes be yet unfurnished of the Bible of the largest volume, the churchwardens shall within convenient time provide the same at the charge of the parish.[14]

The Bible in the Churches

The circulation of the Bishops' Bible at the parish level is told in injunctions, visitation articles, presentments, churchwarden's accounts, and in inventories. The royal injunctions of 1559 had

---

12. Pollard, *Records of the English Bible*, 44.
13. Herbert, *Historical Catalogue*, nos. 185, 186.
14. Phillimore, *Ecclesiastical Law*, 1:926.

ordered each parish to have "one book of the whole Bible of the largest volume in English."[15] The bishops filtered the order down to the parishes. The publication of the Bishops' Bible brought no change in the wording of the injunctions.

Parkhurst in 1559 ordered for Norwich Diocese "A Bible of the largest Volume."[16] Bentham's injunctions (1565) for Coventry and Lichfield varied slightly with "A Bible of the greatest volume."[17]

Grindal's injunctions of 1571 order that children be instructed in the ten commandments and the Lord's Prayer in English,[18] that those above twenty not able to recite the two not be admitted to communion,[19] and that the churchwardens should provide "the English Bible in the largest volume."[20] Grindal's articles of inquiry for Canterbury of 1576 look into these same matters.[21] In the injunctions to the dean and chapter of York, all and every vicar is ordered to have a Bible in English or Latin and to "occupy themselves at times convenient in reading thereof."[22] The articles of inquiry of 1571 investigate compliance.[23]

Horne's injunctions for Winchester College in 1572 ordered:

> Where Latin is not well known ... and also at every meal a chapter of the New Testament shall be openly with a loud voice read in the middle of the hall in English to be heard and understood of the whole company.

In the same year, Guest's articles for Rochester Diocese read:

---

15. Frere and Douglas, *Puritan Manifestoes*, 421; Greenslade, *West from the Reformation*, 159.
16. *STC*, 10289; Frere and Douglas, *Puritan Manifestoes*, 3:210.
17. Frere and Douglas, *Puritan Manifestoes*, 3:170.
18. Nicholson, *Remains of Edmund Grindal*, 124.
19. Ibid., 130.
20. Ibid., 133; Frere and Douglas, *Puritan Manifestoes*, 3:283.
21. Nicholson, *Remains of Edmund Grindal*, 157, 161–62, 163.
22. Ibid., 149; Frere and Douglas, *Puritan Manifestoes*, 3:280.
23. Frere and Douglas, *Puritan Manifestoes*, 3:260.

The Dean of the Cathedral Church and the archdeacon shall have the Bible of the largest volume and the Book of Martyrs set forth.[24]

The wording of articles of visitation after the publication of the Bishops' Bible ordinarily is not different from that used prior to that event. Parker inquired in Canterbury in 1560 after "the Bible in the largest volume,"[25] as did an unknown ordinary in July 1560,[26] and Parkhurst in his area in 1561.[27] Parker also used the same form of inquiry in Norwich in the Metropolitan visitation of 1567.[28]

Figure 15: Exod 25, Ark of the Covenant, "VS" at bottom left (1568).

24. Ibid., 3:336.
25. Ibid., 3:81; Strype, *Life and Acts of Matthew Parker*, 3:28, no. xi.2.
26. Frere and Douglas, *Puritan Manifestoes*, 3:88.
27. Ibid., 3:101.
28. *STC*, 10287.

Sandys's articles for Worcester Diocese in 1569 continued this form and looked for "an English Bible of the greatest volume,"[29] as do Parkhurst's for Norwich.[30] Frek's Articles for Rochester Diocese in 1572–74 inquire of "A faire whole Bible of the largest volume."[31] Parker's articles for Winchester (1575) inquire of "A Bible of the largest volume";[32] Sandys in London, "The English Bible in the largest volume,"[33] and Wickham in Lincoln (1585) are the same.[34] Westfaling for Hereford (1586) demanded "the great English Bible."[35]

On the other hand, Cox in Ely merely sought "whether the parish have a Bible of their own."[36] Also, Robert, bishop of Winchester, in 1570 sought of churchwardens that the parish have "a Bible of their owne, of the largest volume."[37]

Exceptions in the wording of the demand are to be found in the articles of Bishop Bickley for Chichester in 1586 which read, "The English Bible in the largest volume which now is authorized by consent of the Bishops of this realm";[38] and Aylmer in London sought "A Bible of the largest volume of the edition set forth by the bishops and lately imprinted by the Queen's printer, as by letters sent the last year from my Lord's Grace of Canterbury to that effect was enjoined you."[39]

The archdeacon of Norwich in 1601 sought "the English Bible of the largest volume,"[40] as did the archdeacon of Colchester in 1607.[41]

29. Frere and Douglas, *Puritan Manifestoes*, 3:225.
30. STC, 10289.
31. Frere and Douglas, *Puritan Manifestoes*, 3:340.
32. Ibid., 3:281.
33. Ibid., 3:303.
34. Kennedy, *Elizabethan Episcopal Administration*, 188.
35. Ibid., 227.
36. Frere and Douglas, *Puritan Manifestoes*, 3:301.
37. STC, 10352.
38. Kennedy, *Elizabethan Episcopal Administration*, 210.
39. Ibid., 203. See Peel, *Seconde Parte of a Register*, 220.
40. STC, 10301.
41. Ibid., 10188.8.

The later transition in the churches from the Bishops' Bible to the King James Version can be seen in the same sort of sources, with many examples of the same leniency. John, bishop of London in 1615, inquired for a "large Bible of the last edition."[42] Samuel, bishop of Norwich, inquired in 1620 after "a Bible of the largest volume, and of the last translation."[43]

On the other hand, others continued as they had since Edward's time. The archdeacon of Norwich in 1618 asked for "A Bible of the largest volume."[44] Thomas, bishop of Coventry and Lichfield, in 1620 merely sought for "the whole Bible of the largest volume,"[45] as did William, archbishop of Canterbury, in 1638.[46] The demands of William, archbishop of Canterbury in 1635[47] and 1637,[48] of the archdeacon of York in 1635,[49] of Brian Duppa, bishop of Chichester in 1638,[50] as well as of John, bishop of Saint Asaph, as late as 1638 were merely, "Have you a Bible of the largest volume?"[51]

Richard Montague, archdeacon of Hereford, inquired in 1620 for "the whole Bible in English of the largest volume, lately set forth by his maiesties authoritie";[52] but in 1638 as Bishop of Norwich, he inquired for "a Bible of the largest volume and biggest letter."[53]

A notable case arose at Bathealton, where at the visitation of September 1623 it was discovered "that there wanteth a sufficient and decent church bible of the new translation." Nicholas Rew, churchwarden, was cited on September 15 and was given until

42. Ibid., 10259.
43. Ibid., 10293.
44. Ibid., 10301.2.
45. Ibid., 10227.
46. Ibid., 10245.
47. Ibid., 10164.
48. Ibid., 10171.2.
49. Ibid., 10382.5.
50. Ibid., 10185.
51. Wing, *Short-Title Catalogue*, C4082.2.
52. *STC*, 10218.8; Fincham, *Visitation Articles*, 2:194.
53. *STC*, 10299.

January 30 to certify that the needed Bible had been supplied. The case came up again on January 30, February 13, March 13, and April 6, at which time Rew was absolved.[54] The archdeacon of Glocester in 1624 sought the "great Bible of the last Translation."[55] Matthew, bishop of Norwich, in 1626 asked for "the whole Bible in the largest volume of the last translation,"[56] and Matthew, bishop of Ely, in 1538 asked the same.[57] Birchington in 1618 affirms, "We have a . . . Bible."[58] The representative of Capitulum Southwell affirms, "That church hath Bibles."[59]

Throughout the Elizabethan period in these visitations, some churches, though cited for deficiencies, affirm their sufficiency in Bibles. Other parishes were found wanting. In the diocese of York, Kyrkbye in 1570 has no "byble."[60] Also, Weaverham in 1575 lacks a Bible of the largest volume.[61] Brompton in 1595-96 is cited, "Ther Bible is in some ruyne."[62] Skeffling has none,[63] while at Wharleton, "the Byble is not sufficiente."[64] At Ayton, John Topham is cited "for not payinge his cesmente towards the buyinge of a Byble."[65]

Bishop Barnes of Durham finds Simondburne lacking a Bible, October 16, 1579.[66] At Norton in 1580, "There Bible is not sufficient, beinge old and torne, lacking fower or five leaves together in sundrye places of St. Paules epistels." The need is supplied, and the case is dismissed.[67]

54. Jenkins, *Act Book of the Archdeacon*, 45, 154, 159, 162, 170, 175.
55. STC, 10213.8.
56. Ibid., 10298.
57. Ibid., 10197.
58. Hussey, "Visitations of the Archdeacon," (1902) 15.
59. Purvis, *Tudor Parish Documents*, 46.
60. Ibid., 64.
61. Ibid.
62. Ibid., 42.
63. Ibid., 59.
64. Ibid., 51.
65. Ibid., 49.
66. *Injunctions and Other Ecclesiastical Proceedings*, 125.
67. Ibid., 127.

Bishop Redmond of Norwich's visitation in 1579 finds no Bibles at all at Gunton,[68] Bramford,[69] and Ipswich Saint Stephen.[70] The Bramford wardens were excommunicated for lack of compliance. The Bible of the "largest volume" is wanting at Barningham Town,[71] Fincham Saint Michael,[72] Browburg,[73] Felixstowe,[74] Metton,[75] Norfolk,[76] and Swainthorpe.[77]

The wardens of Metton are ordered to buy a Bible by December 8,[78] but the wardens of Felixstowe were excommunicated for noncompliance.[79] The wardens of Blakeney are evasive on the question, stating that they do not know whether their Bible is the largest volume.[80] At Ipswich Saint Nicholas, there was "an olde greate byble."[81] At South Elmham All Saints, "The bible is decayed,"[82] while at Norton Subcourse, "the bible wanteth a cover." In this last case, the wardens said "that they have provided a byble which Mr. Lewger said to be a verie feyer one."[83]

The archdeacon of Canterbury finds at Herne in 1569 that "The Bible is torn and broken in divers places,"[84] and Saint John's in Thanet (Margate) admits "we lack a Bible in the largest volume."[85] In

68. Ibid., 124.
69. Ibid., 146.
70. Ibid., 158.
71. Ibid., 79.
72. Ibid., 92.
73. Ibid.
74. Ibid., 143.
75. Ibid., 78.
76. Ibid., 97.
77. Ibid., 103.
78. Ibid., 78.
79. Ibid., 143.
80. Ibid., 55.
81. Ibid., 157.
82. Ibid., 122.
83. Williams, *Diocese*, 111.
84. Hussey, "Visitations of the Archdeacon," (1902) 26.
85. Ibid., (1904) 17.

1585, Seasalter affirms, "We have a fair bible, but not the same which is called the Bishops' bible."[86] Accounts of Crundal in Kent in 1885 have the entry, "Paid for lack of a Bible at Canterbury . . . 1s. 3d."[87]

The problem of Bibles in the churches continues on into the reign of James. Reculver in 1614 lacks a Bible, and in February 1614–15, the churchwarden appears to affirm that he has provided a Bible.[88]

---

86. Ibid., (1905) 214.

87. "Extracted from an Old Parish Book, Belonging to the Parish of Crundal in Kent," in Somers, *Somers Tracts*, 1:109.

88. Hussey, "Visitations of the Archdeacon," (1902) 44–48.

4

"They Have Bought a Newe Bible"

THE SECOND ROYAL INJUNCTIONS of Henry VIII (1538) ordered setting up of the Bible in the churches with the cost "rateably borne between you, the parson, and the parishioners aforesaid, that is to say, the one half by you, and the other half by them."[1] The move toward compliance is promptly reflected in the churchwardens' accounts. Saint Margaret, Westminster, in 1539, "paid for the half-part of the Bybell accordingly after the King's injunction . . . ixs. ixd."[2] The Tintinhull wardens enter in 1541–42, "It. for the halfe price of the Bible this year bought vj s. v d."[3] Saint Mary the Great, Cambridge, was a frequent purchaser, paying two shillings and six pence for "half the Byble" in 1536, nine shillings in 1540, and seven in 1548. Two shillings were received for sale of "halfe the byble" in 1540, and in 1552 they "payed to Mr. Mayer for the byball wych was strayned the x da of July" three shillings and four pence.[4]

Edward VI in 1547 ordered each parish to provide "one book of the whole Bible of the largest volume in English," which injunction was repeated under Elizabeth in 1559.[5] Ludlow, Shropshire, in 1548 entered under expenditures, "for an edge to stay the Byble upon the deske ij d." and "for a Bible for our partt vij s. viij d." At

1. Gee and Hardy, *Documents Illustrative*, 275–76.
2. Smith, J. E., *Catalogue of Westminster Records*, 44.
3. Hobhouse, *Churchwardens' Accounts*, 205.
4. Foster, J., *Churchwardens' Accounts*, 91–93, 117, 124.
5. Gee and Hardy, *Documents Illustrative*, 421.

the same year, they sold "our part of the olde Byble" for three shillings and four pence.[6]

Grindal's injunctions for the laity specified that the churchwardens "are responsible for providing the English Bible in the largest volume."[7] The continuing purchase of Bibles in the early reign of Elizabeth can be traced. Saint Mary's Cambridge in 1561 enters, "Item a byble bossid xiij s iiij d."[8]

With the issuing of Matthew Parker's Bible, parishes acquired new Bibles, and in some instances sold the old one. Ludlow, Shropsire, accounts enter for 1569, "payd for the exchange of a new Bible, to John Dalton . . . xx s."[9] Saint Martin-in-the-Fields, Westminster, in 1571–72 paid thirty shillings "for a greate newe byble of the laste translation"[10] and purchased another Bible at the same price in 1593, which price equaled the quarter's wages paid to both clerk and sexton.[11]

Ordinarily, the accounts do not specify the version of Scripture purchased. They do reveal, however, that church Bibles lasted a long time and that, though expensive, they were not a major portion of the budget. Some parishes may have been spared the expenditure by gifts from interested parishioners. One bequest of Edmund Grindal was: "To the use of the parish church of St. Bees . . . my fairest English Bible, of the translation appointed to be read in the church."[12] Accounts of Saint Michael's Parish Church, Bishop's Stortford, furnish an interesting history and one pence in 1542 "for a new bybill and the bryngyng home of it." In 1569, they paid "for a new byble" thirty shillings and also bought a "communion boke" and paid four pence "for bringing them home from Cambridge." In 1579–80, they paid twelve pence "for bossing of the byble and stringing of the same byble and communion booke."

6. Wright, *Churchwardens' Accounts*, 37.
7. Quoted in Purvis, *Tudor Parish Documents*, 183.
8. Foster, J., *Churchwardens' Accounts*, 147.
9. Wright, *Churchwardens' Accounts*, 136.
10. Kitto, *Saint Martin-in-the-Fields*, 264.
11. Ibid., 462.
12. Nicholson, *Remains of Edmund Grindal*, 460.

In 1585, they paid eight pence "when we bought in to the court the byble and communion booke to shewe before the comysary." In 1586, they entered, "pd for mending the Byble and communion booke being torne and rent and for clasping of them and for mending the pulpit clothe and paynts xij d." Finally, in 1612 they bought another: "Pd for a new Bible and the carriage of it from London xlviij s. vii d."[13]

Another interesting history is that of Saint Martins, Leicester. In 1548–49, this parish paid "for ij chenes & naylle for the bybell" five pence. In 1559–60, they "Pd to Wm. Shygleton for a bible & a paraphrases" three shillings and four pence. The next year, they paid to "John Ynge for ij chenes & ij staples for the byble and paraphrases" nine pence. Then in 1968–69, they enter, "itm pd to meast comyssarye for a byble xxiij s." Also for this year is entered, "Itm payd to Mr Comyssarye when we was suspended for Lackynge a Byble & to his officers xxiij d." In 1573, the Bible needed repair and so, "itm payd for mendyn of ye old byble to Wille Shypp iij s iiij d." Twelve years later, in a similar entry: "Itm pyd to Godfree Couper for new bindings of the great bible in the church v s. iij d." and also "payd for silke stringes for the same bible vj d." In 1597, the Bible was traded in: "Pyd to Iohn Langford for a New Bybll in money x s. and ovne ovld Bible vallved at vij s. xvi d." Finally, in 1621, "Itm payde for a new bible xl s."[14]

In the vestry minutes for Saint Michael, Cornhill, London, for 1568 is entered, "Item yt ys agreed by ye same vestry yt ye Churche wardens shal by a faire Byble." The wardens complied, and their accounts have the entry: "Itm paide for the Newe Byble xxvij s." In 1573, an entry of sixteen pence is made for "claspes and bosses for the greate Bible," but it was not until 1591 that a new Bible was acquired at a cost of thirty shillings. The proceedings of the vestry for June 20, 1596, read: "It is ordred that the Saxton shall after service don pntely carry in the Bible and service books to the vestry to be locked for the better saffetie of them and that the

---

13. Glasscock, *Records of St. Michael's*, 43, 56, 60, 63, 64, 68.

14. North, *Accounts of the Church Wardens*, 40, 88, 91, 116, 123, 129, 140, 162.

Church dore shalbe kept shut in the week daies after service times whereby boys and others maie be kept forth frome doeing damage." A further entry is made by the wardens in 1597 for "bossinge & claspinge the Bible" which cost two shillings.[15]

Other interesting purchases of Bibles in 1568–69 include the Lambeth parish, which paid twenty-six shillings and eight pence "for a new bible of the greatest volume." However, a "Mr. John Porye Doctor od Dyvynitie and parson of Lamb" paid half this sum so that the parish was out only thirteen shillings and four pence. In this same year, "one daies worke about the little gate and mending ij pewes" cost two shillings.[16] Ludlow parish in 1569 paid twenty shillings "for the exchange of a New bible to John Dalton."[17] Saint John, Winchester, in 1568–69 paid thirteen shillings and four pence for a new Bible and received six shillings for an old one.[18] Records of Saint John's College, Cambridge, reveal that in 1571, the college paid "for a new Bible in English the last translation 27s 8d."[19]

On May 4, 1572, Holy Trinity, Chester, paid twenty-eight shillings "for a great bible to serve the church."[20] All Hallows, Staining, paid the same amount in 1575, and the warden, W. Yvesey, entered ten shillings in receipts "for the owld bible wh I tak for my selfe."[21] Saint Nicholas Strood reports in 1571–74, "Rec of Goodman James for the great byble ix s." and "Item paid for Fetching of the bible more than I did receive ij s. iiij d." A "Byble of the largest volume" is then inventoried in 1574, 1576, 1582–83, 1592, but "one church bible" in 1607 and 1612, after which time, in 1619, a new Bible is purchased.[22]

---

15. Overall, *Accounts of the Churchwardens*, 236, 163, 167, 253, 187.
16. Drew, *Lambeth Churchwardens' Accounts*, 97.
17. Wright, *Churchwarden's Account*, 140.
18. Cox, *Churchwardens' Accounts*, 118.
19. Hartshorne, *Book Rarities*, 333.
20. Beresford, "Churchwardens' Accounts," 127.
21. Povah, *Annals of the Parishes*, 364.
22. Plomer, *Churchwardens' Accounts*, 28, 33, 36, 56, 71, 107, 119.

Figure 16: Exod 29, Aaron as priest, "VS" at bottom left of priest, "SH" at bottom right of priest (1568).

In 1576 or 1577, Saint Helen's, Abingdon, paid forty shillings "for a new byble."[23] Their previous purchase had been in 1562 at a cost of ten shillings. In 1578, Stanford-in-the-Vale, Berkshire, paid twenty-two shillings and an additional seven pence "for brynging the sayd byble from oxford."[24] Cratfield paid twenty-four shillings two pence "for a Bible for the church" in 1583.[25] The next year (1585), Shillington paid thirty-six shillings six pence.[26] Howden paid twenty shillings in 1594 "for one bibell for the churche."[27] In 1590, Exning, Suffolk, "Paid for the byble at London and for bringinge of yt from the Stationers to my ende" twenty-eight shillings two pence.[28] In 1591, Saint Nicholas Parish, Warwickshire, "also

23. Nichols, *Illustrations of the Manners*, 143.
24. Haines, "Stanford Churchwardens' Accounts," 171.
25. Holland, *Cratfield: Transcript of the Accounts*, 108.
26. Farmiloe and Nixseaman, *Elizabethan Churchwardens' Accounts*, 81.
27. Weddall, "Churchwardens' Accounts," 458.
28. Cox, *Churchwardens' Accounts*, 118.

the saide accompsats have pd for a newe Bible for the church xxx s."[29] In 1602–3, Northill, Bedfordshire, paid forty-one shillings six pence "for a Bible and a common prayer booke."[30]

In 1592, the wardens of the Warrington Parish are accused, "They wante the Bible . . .," but the wardens appear to affirm "that they have bought a newe Bible."[31] Charge is made against the Aughton Parish, "there bible is not sufficient." Two wardens appear and are enjoined to buy a "sufficient bible."[32] Saint Elben's Chapel is found to lack all the books mentioned in the visitation articles.[33]

In 1595, Wilton is charged: "they have a meane byble, and it is not in the largest volume."[34]

Redenhall, in 1596, paid "at London for a byble & the carriage of the same" thirty-three shillings four pence, and one "ould byble was sould vnto Baxter by Jas. Thomson" for ten shillings.[35]

Some churches during this period purchased Geneva Bibles. Acaster Malbis Parish in Yorkshire in 1575 is accused: "They have a Geneva bible, but not of the largest volume."[36] In 1578, Saint Mary's the Great, Cambridge, paid seventeen shillings for "an englyshe geneva bible." In the inventory of 1583, there appears "one Jeneva bible."[37]

Having the Bible in the churches involved other expenditures. Saint Martin-in-the-Fields in 1571–72 "payde for torninge a pyller to Sett the byble one viij d." and "for altering the Ironworke to sett the byble on ij s. v d."[38]

During the reigns of Henry VIII and Edward VI, numerous entries in the wardens's accounts are for chains, for the Bible was

29. Savage, *Churchwardens' Accounts*, 85.
30. Farmiloe and Nixseaman, *Elizabethan Churchwardens' Accounts*, 46.
31. Irvine, "Visitation of Warrington Deanery," 191.
32. Ibid., 184.
33. Ibid., 185.
34. Fallow, "Some Elizabethan Visitations," 204.
35. Chandler, *Notes on the Parish of Redenhall*, 65.
36. Skaife, "Extracts from the Visitation," 224.
37. Foster, J., *Churchwardens' Accounts*, 191, 205.
38. Kitto, *Saint Martin-in-the-Fields*, 256.

chained to the desk in the churches. In 1539, Patton churchwardens "Payd to J Meryfyld for makyng a cheyne to ye bybyll . . . viijd.,"[39] and in 1542, Tintinhull paid three pence "for a chayne to hold the Bible."[40] All Hallows, Staining, London, in 1540 bought a Bible for eleven shillings eight pence and paid "for byndding ther of and a chayne" three shillings one pence. Also, there was sent "for a lok and ij keyse for the avmbre (closet) under the bible, and ij henge" sixteen pence.[41] Chaining in the university libraries continued until late in the eighteenth century. At Magdalen College, Oxford, they were not removed until 1799.[42]

During the period of Elizabeth, these older Bibles remained chained in some of the churches; but in addition, some new Bibles were also chained. On November 15, 1578, the officials of the Hospital of Saint Thomas of Acorn approved the purchase of a Bible "to stand and remain without in the hall, the same to be bossed and fast chained in some convient place there."[43] Saint Michael, Cornhill, London, in 1591, "Paide for chaynes & for a locke & nayles for the bookes in ye Churche" fifteen pence.[44] The inventory of Saint Margaret for 1614–15 has "one deske with an ould Bible fastened to it."[45] The copy of the Bishops' Bible owned by the library no longer has its chains but has the holes in the cover where they were attached. Wimborne Minster, Dorset, still has its Bishops' Bible of the year 1595 chained to its stand.[46]

A certain amount of wear and tear was involved in the use of the Bible. Rebinding is a frequent expenditure. Saint John the Baptist, Peterborough, paid twenty pence in 1570–73 "for finding and covering the Bible."[47] Cheswarding Parish entered for 1574, "for

39. Hobhouse, *Churchwardens' Accounts*, 153.
40. Ibid., 205.
41. Povah, *Annals of the Parishes*, 363.
42. Streeter, *Chained Library*, xiv.
43. Watney, *Some Account of the Hospital*, 167.
44. Overall, *Accounts of the Churchwardens*, 182.
45. Smith, J.E., *Catalogue of Westminster Records*, 241.
46. Blades, *Books in Chains*, 12.
47. Mellows, *Peterborough Local Administration*, 175.

"They Have Bought a Newe Bible"

leaves to amend our byble xvi d-" and "to Harrie eldershowe for byndyng the bible in*- ix 4- d." A few years later, in 1579, they sold the "old byble" for five shillings six pence and entered a payment "for the byble & the caryage xxi*s." Much later, in 1613 is entered, "for ye mending of or. bible and my charges to fetch itt and bring itt to Shrewsbury x s. xi d."[48] The accounts of the Travistock, Devonshire, Parish Church has for 1588–89: "Paide William Trenaman for Three chaynes of Ire with plates and for the fastenynge of the Bible, Paraphras of Erasmus and Mr. Juell's Booke in the churche . . . iijs. ijd."[49]

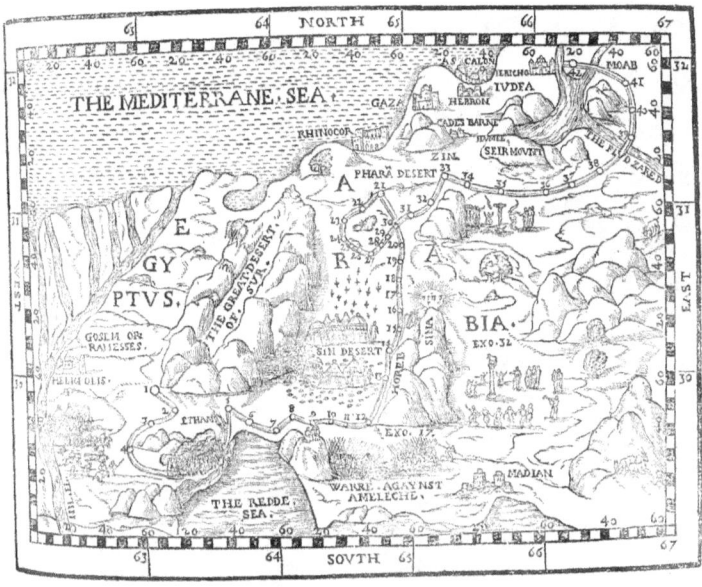

Figure 17: Map, way of the people of Israel in the wilderness, Num 33 (1568).

In 1570-71, Saint Thomas, Sarum, paid "2/1/6 for a greate Bible," and then in 1573-74 paid "Harry Hamon seting of boses on ye bybyll and 2 large strapes also for the savings of him" two

48. Hughes, "Cheswardine Churchwardens' Account," 65–66, 73.
49. Cited in Blades, *Books in Chains*, 72–73.

75

shillings six pence.[50] In 1587, for "mendingne ye byble," two shillings.[51] Saint Edmonds in 1597–98 paid four shillings six pence to "ye booke binder for mending of the Church byble."[52] Saint Mary's the Great, Cambridge, in 1601 paid "for mendinge ye greate Church bible with bosses and clasps and bufinge ye backe" one shilling four pence.[53] Kilmington, East Devonshire, in 1591–92 "payd for lacynge for the byble" two pence.[54] Cratfield spent seven shillings ten pence in 1604 for rebinding "of a Bible & of Erasmuses Epitaphs."[55]

50. Cox, *Churchwardens' Accounts*, 118.
51. Swayne, *Churchwardens' Accounts*, 297.
52. Ibid., 146.
53. Foster, J., *Churchwardens' Accounts*, 281.
54. Cornish, *Kilmington Churchwardens' Accounts*, 75.
55. Holland, *Cratfield: Transcript of the Accounts*, 139.

5

Influence of the Bishops' Bible

Shakespeare and the Bishops' Bible

RICHMOND NOBLE HAS CONVINCINGLY demonstrated that William Shakespeare, contrary to popular opinion, often in his earlier plays reflects a use of the Bishops' Bible and the Prayer Book,[1] while the later plays reflect the Geneva Version.[2] Shakespeare's total usage of Scripture includes quotations or allusions from forty-two books of the Bible.[3] While some Scriptures used read alike in the Geneva and Bishops' versions, others are unique to the Bishops'. Noble points out that the echoes of the Bishops' are most abundant in *Love's Labour's Lost*, where passages from Judges, Ecclesiastes, Song of Solomon, Jeremiah, Luke, and Romans occur. Not one of the Old Testament chapters is a part of a lesson read in the churches on Sundays.[4] How Shakespeare came by this knowledge is a matter of conjecture. By 1588–89 when the first play, *The Comedy of Errors*, appeared, there had already been seven folio and five quarto editions of the Bishops' Bible. It would not have been impossible for him to have owned a copy.

While in many items a decision of versions cannot be made, some of the cases adduced by Noble for the Bishops' in the order of their occurrence in Scripture are as follows:

1. Noble, *Shakespeare's Biblical Knowledge.*
2. Ibid., 44.
3. Ibid., 20, 21.
4. Ibid., 73.

77

1. Judg 16:8 — "withs that were yet greene." *Love's Labour's Lost*, I.ii.95.[5]
2. 2 Kgs 4:26 — "all is well." *Romeo and Juliet*, IV.v.76; *Henry IV, Part 2*, V.ii.3; *Macbeth*, IV.iii.176–79; *Anthony and Cleopatra*, II.v.32–33; *The Winter's Tale*, V.i.30.[6]
3. Job 33:6; cf. Tob 8:8 — "made even of the same moulde." *Richard II*, I.ii.22–24.[7]
4. Prov 1:20–24 — "Wysdome cryeth . . . in the streetes . . . and no man regarded." *Henry IV, Part 1*, I.ii.99–100.[8]
5. Eccl 12:9, 12 — "All is but vanitie (saith the preacher) all is but plaine vanitie . . . too much study wearieth the body." *Love's Labour's Lost*, I.i.70–75.[9]
6. Song 1:4–5 — "I am blacke (O ye daughters of Hierusalem) but yet fayre." *Love's Labour's Lost*, IV.iii.246–53.[10]
7. Song 5:10 — "My loue, he is white and red coloured." *Love's Labour's Lost*, I.ii.96.[11]
8. Jer 13:23 — "A man of Inde." *Love's Labour's Lost*, IV.iii.222; *The Tempest*, II.ii.61.[12]
9. Tob 5:23; 10:4 — "The staffe of our age." *The Merchant of Venice*, II.ii.71–72.[13]
10. Eccl 28:4 — "You must not dare . . . to talk of mercy."[14]

---

5. Ibid., 71.
6. Ibid., 75.
7. Ibid., 74–75.
8. Ibid., 25, 74.
9. Ibid., 71, 143.
10. Ibid., 72, 145.
11. Ibid., 72.
12. Ibid., 71, 72, 145.
13. Ibid., 73, 164.
14. Ibid.

11. Matt 20:16 — "Harmelesse as the Doues." *Henry IV, Part 2*, III.i.69–71.[15]
12. Matt 28:9 — "All haile." *Love's Labour's Lost*, V.ii.340.[16]
13. Luke 6:23 — "And leape ye for ioy"; cf. Isa 35:6. *Love's Labour's Lost*, V.ii.292.[17]
14. Luke 6:26 — "Woe vnto you when men shal prayse you." *Twelfth Night*, V.i.19.[18]
15. Rom 13:10 — "Charitie worketh no ill to his neighbor, therefore the fulfyllyng of the lawe is charitie." *Love's Labour's Lost*, IV.iii.363–65; *Titus Andronicus*, V.ii.43; *The Merchant of Venice*, I.ii.84.[19]
16. Eph 5:16; Col 4:5 — "Redeeming the time." *King Henry IV, Part 1*, I.ii.239(187).[20]
17. Phil 1:21 — "Death is to him advantage." *Henry V*, IV.i.193.[21]
18. 1 Pet 4:3 — "in excesse of wines." *Henry V*, II.ii.42.[22]
19. Rev 3:5 — "and I wil not blot out his name out of the booke of life." *Richard II*, I.ii.202.[23]

A second category of influence on Shakespeare, in addition to that of the text, is from the marginal notes of the Bishops' Bible. Ginsburg and Noble have called attention to the note of Genesis 31:9, "It is not lawefull by fraude to seke recompence of iniurie: therefore Moyses sheweth afterwards that God thus instructed Jacob," influenced Antonio's remark in *The Merchant of Venice* I.ii,

---

15. Ibid., 70.
16. A case of error on Shakespeare's part. Ibid., 103–4.
17. But also in Geneva margin. Ibid., 73, 146–47.
18. Ibid., 75.
19. Ibid., 770–71. Ginsburg, "Shakespeare's Use of the Bible," 542.
20. Noble, *Shakespeare's Biblical Knowledge*, 74, 171.
21. Ibid., 75.
22. Ibid., 74.
23. Ibid., 73.

that the matter was God's wonderful interposition and must not be adduced as justifying foul play.[24]

Figure 18: Gen 3, Adam and Eve in the garden with animals, serpent in tree at center top, "SH" at left lower third of picture (1568).

"My story" (*Henry VI, Part* 2, II.ii.25) and "Pangs of death" (frequently used) are from Psalm 18:3; 2 Samuel 22:5.[25]

Shakespeare echoes the Psalms frequently. Noble found these, with two exceptions, to echo the Prayer Book version. Even here, one must reckon with influence from Bishops' printings, which in 1572 had the two Psalm versions side by side and after 1585 only printed the Great Bible Psalms. Though the Prayer Book itself is an equally likely source, if Shakespeare had heard or read any Bishops' Bible except the 1568, 1569, 1572, or 1585 editions, he would have heard the Prayer Book Psalms. From this source comes "My

---

24. Ginsburg, "Shakespeare's Use of the Bible," 541.

25. The latter is also in the Geneva Bible. Noble, *Shakespeare's Biblical Knowledge*, 25.

heart skippeth for joy" (*The Winter's Tale*, I.ii.111-12; cf. Ps 28:8) and "Fall away like water" (*Henry VIII*, II.i.128-30).[26]

This knowledge is not without its errors. In the Bishops' Bible, "all haile" (as also in the Tyndale and the Great Bible) is on the lips of Jesus as he greets the women after the resurrection (Matt 28:9), but is used by Shakespeare for the greeting of Judas (Matt 26:49) in *Henry VI, Part 3*, V.vii.33-34 and in *Richard II*, IV.ii.169, though no version so used it. The greeting of the Master has been transferred to the betrayer (cf. *Love's Labour's Lost*, V.ii.340).[27]

Turning to the use of names, Iacob (*The Merchant of Venice*, I.iii.72, *et seq.*)[28] and Chus (*The Merchant of Venice*, III.ii.286)[29] from Genesis 10 are spelled as in the Bishops' Bible. Less conclusive evidence is the use of "Saba" for Sheba (*Henry VIII*, V.v.25-26), which might also have come either from Geneva page and chapter headings or from the Vulgate.[30] Noble puts even less confidence in arguments from spelling of names like "Achitophel" (2 Sam 15-17) since the Bishops' versions are not consistent on the question.[31]

Items in common with the Geneva Bible but not with the Thomson revision include 1 Corinthians 7:14 — "The vnbeleeuing wife is sanctified by the husbande" in *The Merchant of Venice*, III.v.21.[32]

Items in which it is likely but not certain that the Bible is being echoed include Genesis 19:30 — "Come unto us after the manner of all the world" (for marriage) in *Much Ado About Nothing*, II.i.332; *All's Well That Ends Well*, I.iii.20; *As You Like It*, V.iii.4-5.[33]

26. Ibid., 79-80.
27. Ibid., 103-4.
28. Ibid., 268-70.
29. Ibid., 104-5.
30. Ibid., 70.
31. Ibid., 261.
32. Ibid., 73.
33. Ibid., 29.

Items not from the Geneva Bible that could be either from the Bishops' Bible or the Prayer Book are "Judean,"[34] and "Jewry,"[35] and Matthew 16:18 — "The gates of hel shall not prevaile against it" in *Henry VI, Part 1*, I.v.9.[36]

The Bishops' Bible in America

While the English exploration and early efforts at colonization of America took place during the period of the circulation of the Bishops' Bible, that Bible, which appeared in its last folio edition in 1602, was rapidly being displaced in church usage by the King James Version before the landing of the Mayflower at Plymouth in 1620 and before the floodtide of colonization set in. In addition, the popularity of the Geneva Bible with many colonists has long been known. The extent of the role played by the Bishops' Bible in the early American colonies, through scarcity of concrete examples, is indeed problematic. Nevertheless, Marion Simms has shown that most of the evidence, though inferential rather than explicit, carries some degree of probability.[37]

The chaplain of Sir Francis Drake, Francis Fletcher, conducted Anglican services in June 1579 on the California coast when the expedition put in to a "convenient and fit harbor" for repairs. The service included prayers, "singing of psalms, and reading of certain chapters in the Bible."[38] Those misled by the popular, sweeping generalization that the Bishops' Bible was used in the churches and that the Geneva Bible was used at home and those familiar only with the heavy Bishops' folios printed in 1568 and 1572 rightly feel certain that explorers are not likely to have carried such Bibles with them. It should be remembered, however, that in 1578, when Drake's expedition sailed, five quarto editions of the

---

34. Ibid., 70, 273.
35. Ibid., 70, 271.
36. Ibid., 70, 32.
37. Simms, *Bible in America*, 72–82.
38. *STC*, 7161, 32.

Bishops' Bible and perhaps as many as nine New Testaments, all portable, had been issued. Furthermore, the small folio Bible of 1575,[39] approximately eleven by seven and one-half by two inches in size, is as portable as an *Encyclopedia Britannica* volume. At the same time, quarto editions of the Great Bible were issued in 1553, 1561, 1568, and 1569. This Bible, as we have seen, had not been declared unfit for use by good Anglicans. There had been by 1578 only two quarto editions of the Geneva Bible (1560 and 1570), four folio (1562, 1576, 1576, and 1577), and one octavo edition (1577). There had been numerous portable New Testaments of the various versions issued. In the absence of further evidence, that the expedition had a Bishops' Bible remains only a possibility.

Martin Frobisher, who on his third voyage as expedition commander for Sir Humphrey Gilbert first led an English colony to America, had in his "Orders to be observed for the Fleete" instructions "to serue God twice a day with the ordinary seruice usuall in the churches of England."[40] Departing Norwich on May 27, 1583, among a hundred colonists was Maister Wolfall appointed to be their "Minister and Preacher." Gilbert's patent provided that he establish "the true Christian faith or religion now professed in the Church of England." On Sunday, August 4, 1583, Frobisher took formal possession of Saint John's Newfoundland and enjoined that the service of religion should be "in the publique exercise according to the Church of England."[41]

Wolfall's service on this expedition gained for him the distinction of being the first missionary priest of the reformed Church of England who ministered on American shores.[42] Late in August, "Maister Wolfall on Winter's Fornace, preached a godly sermon" and "celebrated also a Communion upon the land." Wolfall also "made sermons, and celebrated the Communion at sundry other times, in seuerall and sundry ships, because the whole company

---

39. Ibid., 2110–2113a.

40. Hakluyt, *Principal Navigations*, 3:75 (STC, 12626x). Cf. Perry, *Connection of the Church*, 3.

41. Perry, *Connection of the Church*, 4.

42. Perry, *History of the American*, 1:6–7.

could neuer meet together in any one place."⁴³ We would assume, in the lack of specific evidence, that Wolfall, "a true Pastor and Minister of God's Word," with his aim "to saue soules, and to reforme these infidels if it were possible to Christianitie," certainly had a Bible.

Sir Humphrey Gilbert, returning to England from Newfoundland, was reading an unidentified book, conjectured to be a Bible, on the deck of the overloaded ship, Squirrel, during a storm on the day prior to the disappearance of the Squirrel in the night of September 9, 1583.⁴⁴

Neither Drake, Gilbert, nor their chaplains are thought to have had Puritan leanings, which would cause them to favor the Geneva Bible. Though their Bibles—assuming that they had them—could have been one of the printings of the Great Bible, which we have earlier mentioned, they need not have been so.

The first colony specifically known to have had a Bible is that of Sir Walter Raleigh in North Carolina. There, Thomas Hariot, a member of the colonists at Roanoke Island led by Ralph Lane in 1585, displayed a Bible to the Indians and attempted to teach them from it. The Indians, despite Hariot's teaching to the contrary, superstitiously regarded the book as having magical qualities and kissed it and touched their bodies with it.⁴⁵ By this time, there had been six quarto and seven folio printings of the Bishops' Bible.

The colony led by George Popham at Kennebec River, Maine, in 1607, had along with them Richard Seymour as preacher. On August 9, they landed on "St. Georges Island" and "there had a Sermon deliver'd them by their Preacher," reports the expedition's chronicler, "giving God thanks for our happy and safe arrival into the country."⁴⁶ Still farther up the river on Wednesday, August 19:

> We made choice for our plantation, and there we had a sermon delivered to us by our preacher, and after the

---

43. Hakluyt, *Principal Navigations*, 3:91; Perry, *Connection of the Church*, 4.

44. Hakluyt, *Principal Navigations*, 3:159.

45. STC, 1285, fol. E 4; cf. Smith, J., *Generall Historie of Virginia*, 11 (STC, 22790).

46. Davies, *Relation of a Voyage*, 27; cf. Strachey, *Historie of Travell*, 165.

sermon our patent was read with the orders and laws therein prescribed.⁴⁷

The group constructed a fort, houses, and a church building.⁴⁸ On October 4, two canoes of Indians came to the fort and were "feasted and entertained with all kyndnes both that day and the next, which being Sonday the President carried them with him to the place of publique prayers, which they were at both morning and evening, attendying yt with great Revrence and sylence."⁴⁹ The colony was established under the instruction from the king, which provided for worship "according to the doctrine, rights, and religion now professed and established within our realm of England."⁵⁰ John G. Shea conjectured that the Bible used by this group would have been the Bishops' Bible.⁵¹ The colony was abandoned after one winter.

Only slightly earlier, with the founding of the colony at Jamestown, Robert Hunt,⁵² described by Captain Edward-Maria Wingfield as "a man not any way to be touched with the rebellious humors of popish spirit, nor blemish with ye least suspition of a factius scismatick,"⁵³ came as the preacher. Hunt had been selected for the place by Richard Hakluyt with the concurrence of Richard Bancroft. Hunt celebrated communion on June 21, 1607, which act is credited with being the first such observance by Englishmen in America of which a record remains. A rude church building, which—along with Hunt's library—was shortly to be destroyed by fire, was erected, and then was followed by a new church building in the spring of 1605.⁵⁴ Hunt was described by Captain John Smith

---

47. Davies, *Relation of a Voyage*, 30; cf. Strachey, *Historie of Travell*, 167; and Burrage, *Beginnings of Colonial Maine*, 77.

48. Strachey, *Historie of Travell*, 172–73.

49. Ibid., 172.

50. Brown, *Genesis of the United States*, 1:68.

51. Shea, "Bible in American History," 135.

52. *DAB*, 9:391–92.

53. Wingfield, *Discourse on Virginia*, 102.

54. Purchas, *Hakluytus Posthumus*, 4:1710; Smith, J., *Generall Historie of Virginia*, 52–53.

as "an honest, courageous, religious divine; during whose life our factions were oft qualified, our wants and greatest extremities so comforted that they seemed easier in comparison of what we endured after his memorable death."[55]

Wingfield, first president of the colony, after his return to England, May 21, 1608, defended himself against the charge of not taking a Bible with him on the claim that his Bible had been packed in a trunk and sent to a Mr. Crofts in Ratcliff who had proceeded to embezzle Wingfield's property, and the fate of the Bible he did not know.[56]

A later group of colonists, carried by a storm off their course to Bermuda, on July 28, 1609, observed "public prayer every morning" and on Sunday two sermons were preached by Richard Bucke, "a verie good preacher." The historian of the group reports, "It pleased God also to give us opportunitie, to performe all the other Offices and Rites of our Christian Profession on this Island."[57] The group finally reached Virginia on the twenty-third of May, and there Bucke conducted services,[58] as he also did when De la Warr arrived.[59]

Despite the fact that the Sandys, sons of Edwin Sandys, one of the preparers of the Bishops' Bible, were influential in the Virginia Colony, Simms felt that a Puritan influence using the Geneva Bible was the more dominant influence in the colony.[60] The colonists were sent off to Jamestown with a sermon on April 25, 1609, at White Chapel, "in the presence of . . . the adventuers and planters for Virginia" by Richard Symonds, preacher at Saint Saviours in Southwarke, in which he took his text from Genesis 12:1–3 from the Geneva Bible.[61] The sermon is saturated with other Geneva

55. Burleson, "How Our Church Came to Virginia," in Burleson, *How Our Church Came*, 4.
56. Wingfield, *Discourse on Virginia*, 27–28.
57. Perry, *History of the American*, 1:54.
58. Purchas, *Hakluytus Posthumus*, 4:1746, 1748–49.
59. Ibid., 4:1754.
60. Simms, *Bible in America*, 75–79.
61. STC, 23595, 1, 44.

paraphrases and quotations. In the presence of De la Warr, February 21, 1609, just before the departure of the Gates party, William Crawshaw preached from Luke 22:32 from the Geneva Bible, and the sermon is also saturated with Geneva material.[62] William Strachey, in describing the vicissitudes of Jamestown in 1610, cited Proverbs 6:10–11 from the Geneva Bible.[63]

Figure 19: Gen 7, Noah's ark in the flood, dove at top descending with olive branch, "VS" at bottom left (1568).

Alexander Whitaker, one of the early preachers in Jamestown, wrote to William Gouge, June 18, 1614, "I much more muse that so few of our English ministers that were so hot against the surplice and subscription come hither whether neither is spoken of."[64] Though Whitaker, a son of William Whitaker, a well-known Puritan, regularly used the Geneva Bible, in "good News from Virginia," 1613, after using the text Ecclesiastes 11:1, "Cast thy bread

62. Ibid., 6029.
63. Purchas, *Hakluytus Posthumus*, 4:1749.
64. *DAB*, 20:78–80.

upon the Waters: for after many daies thou shalt finde it," in the Geneva form of this text, used a phrase peculiar to the Bishops' Bible: "he would thrust forth labourers into the harvest" (Matt 9:38 and margin of Luke 10:2).[65]

¶ The ⁽ᵃ⁾ Gofpell by Saint Matthewe.

Figure 20: Evangelist Matthew at opening of his Gospel in 1568 Bible, his symbol the angel, "SF" on chair where Matthew sits.

A slightly earlier evidence for use of the Bishops' Bible is to be seen in an episode involving Captain Samuel Argall. Argall, in 1610, while trading with the Indians of Patawomeck River, had on board a man reading the Bible. Seeing the curiosity about the book on the part of the Indian Iopassus, "the captayne tooke the booke, and turned to the picture of the Creation of the World, in the begynning of the booke, and caused a boy, one Spilman, who had lyved a whole yere with this Indian kinge, and spake his language, to shew yt unto him, and to enterprete yt in his language, which

---

65. *STC*, 25355, 1, 44.

the boy did . . ."⁶⁶ Some printings of the Bishops' Bible carried the picture of the creation at the beginning, whereas the Geneva did not. Even the Bishops' editions did not all carry the same picture. At the beginning of Genesis, the 1568 edition had Eden but had no representation of man, and God is represented only by the Tetragrammaton on the sun.

Figure 21: Gen 1, Garden of Eden, Tetragrammaton on sun, "SH" at bottom left (1568).

In the 1572 edition, followed by the 1573 quarto, a different picture has Adam seated under a tree at the lower left. The 1585, 1595, and 1602 folios have a large picture of Adam and Eve in Paradise, one on each side of the Tree of Knowledge and about fifty animals around them. Hortatory words are written on the branches of the tree.

---

66. Strachey, *Historie of Travell*, 98.

Figure 22: Garden of Eden in Christopher Barker's 1583 folio edition.

This evidence makes it likely that the Bishops' Bible, along with the better-known Geneva Bible, played a role in the earliest colonization of America. Its day had passed before the colonies had developed to the point of printing a Bible. It was not printed in America until Luther Weigle issued *The New Testament Octapla* in 1962 and *The Genesis Octapla* in 1965, in which publications the relevant portion of the Bishops' Bible is one of the eight versions printed.

6

Art in the Bishops' Bible

ARTISTICALLY, THE FIRST EDITION of the Bishops' Bible was a most impressive volume—the most ornate English Bible that had appeared to that date, with no pains spared to make it appealing. Elaborate title pages, engravings, woodcut illustrations, and decorative initials at the beginnings of books and of chapters all added to its elegance. These items varied from edition to edition, and by no means are all editions of equal elegance.

The first edition contained three portraits. The first title page contained a portrait of Queen Elizabeth (see figure 1); the second—that before Joshua—carried a portrait of Dudley, earl of Leicester; and the book of Psalms began with a decorative "B" which included a portrait of William Cecil, Elizabeth's secretary of state, later (February 25, 1570) Lord Burghley, suggesting that Cecil possessed the blessedness described in the first Psalm (see figure 33). Parker's patrons, even in the absence of a specific dedication, are thus placed in flattering positions approximate to Moses, Joshua, and David. All three of these portraits are conjectured to be the work of Franciscus Hogenberg, who had been brought to Lambeth Palace by Parker to aid his publications. Parker mentions that he had "drawers and cutters, paynters, lymmers, wryters, and boke-bynders" in his house "in wagis."[1]

These portraits are also in the 1572 folio; but in that edition, Burghley's picture—an entirely different portrait—is on the title page of Psalms rather than at the beginning of the Psalm in the

---

1. Strype, *Life and Acts of Matthew Parker*, 3:4:269.

position of the Blessed Man.² The portraits do not appear in editions after the third (1572) edition.

Figure 23: Title page to second part of 1568 Bible, portrait of Robert Dudley, Earl of Leicester.

Title Page Borders

Elaborate woodcut compartments (title page borders) make up the title pages of the various five sections of the 1568 edition. These, as McKerrow and Ferguson[3] have shown, were used by Jugge in other publications of this period, as well as their reappearing in some subsequent editions of the Bishops' Bible. The following of these devices are described by McKerrow and Ferguson:

2. Hind, *Engraving in England*, 1:68–69.
3. McKerrow and Ferguson, *Title-Page Borders*.

Art in the Bishops' Bible

100. (159 x 107 mm., enclosing 78 x 47 mm.) A compartment with masks at top and sides, and at foot a nightingale in a thornbush. The MOTTO OMNE. BONV̄. SVPERNAE (= Device 182.).

...

1575 by R. Jugge. *The holy byble* (S.T.C. 2114).
On the title to the second part (sig. O i).
1576 by R. Jugge. *The holy byble* (S.T.C. 2115).
On the general title.[4]

...

1577 by R. Jugge. *The holy byble* (S.T.C. 2121).
On the general title and that to the *New Testament*.[5]

111. (149 x 102 mm., enclosing 83 x 56.5 mm.) A compartment with Richard Jugge's monogram at top, termini at sides, and two lions couchant at foot (= Device 134).

...

[1569] by R. Jugge. *The holi bible.*
Title to *N.T.*, which is dated 1569. The piece with monogram at top is cracked.[6]

127. (173 x 127 mm., enclosing 21 x 61 mm.) A compartment representing Queen Elizabeth enthroned being crowned by 'IVSTICE' and 'MERCIE'; 'FORTITVDE' and 'PRVDENCE' seated below, supporting the throne. Beneath the tablet bearing the title, a man in a pulpit, an hourglass at his side, is preaching to a seated congregation. At the base: GOD SAVE THE QVEENE.

...

[1569] by R. Jugge. *The holi bible.*
The title to the *N.T.* is dated 1569.

...

[1573] by R. Jugge. *The holie byble* (S.T.C. 2108).
On the general title. The tablet is occupied by a quotation from John v. The *New Testament* title is dated 1573.[7]

4. John 5.
5. McKerrow and Ferguson, *Title-Page Borders*, 94.
6. Ibid., 99.
7. See Hind, *Engraving in England*, 1:7.

(ß)The figure of Queen Elizabeth has been voided, leaving an irregular compartment with inner measurement of 72 x 37 (42) mm.
1575 by R. Jugge. *The holy byble* (S.T.C. 2114).
On the general title.
1577 R. Jugge. *The holy byble* (S.T.C. 2122).
On the general title.[8]

129. (291 x 192 mm., enclosing 91 x 78 mm.) A compartment with the Royal Arms at the top and figures of Faith and Charity.[9]
[1568] by R. Jugge. *The holie bible* (S.T.C. 2099).
On the title to the *New Testament*.
1572 by R. Jugge. *The holie bible*.
On the title to the *New Testament*.[10]
1574 (July 5) by R. Jugge. *The holy byble*.
On the general title and that to the *New Testament*.[11]
1578 by the assignement of C. Barker. *The holy byble*.
On the general title and that to the *New Testament*.[12]

141. (162 x 104 mm., enclosing 108 x 59 mm.) A compartment with the Royal Arms at top; a pelican in her piety at foot, with, to left, Cupid (?) holding the letter R, and, to right, a nightingale in a thorn bush, with the word ivgge (= Device 181).

. . .

[1573] by R. Jugge. *The holie byble* (S.T.C. 2108).
On the subtitles to the second and third parts, the *Apocrypha*, and the *New Testament*, which is dated 1573.
1575 by R. Jugge. *The holy byble* (S.T.C. 2114).
On the title to the third part, to the *Apocrypha*, and that to the *New Testament*.

. . .

8. McKerrow and Ferguson, *Title-Page Borders*, 112.

9. See figure 5.

10. Cherubs clinging to foliage at side. Lion and dragon at bottom corners. Oval center. Rom 1:16 quoted on lower plate.

11. General title to each of the Scriptures. John 5:39 on plate.

12. McKerrow and Ferguson, *Title-Page Borders*, 113.

Art in the Bishops' Bible

1576 by R. Jugge. *The holy byble* (S.T.C. 2115).
On the titles to the second and third parts, to the *Apocrypha*, and to the *New Testament*.
1577 by R. Jugge. *The holy bible* (S.T.C. 2121).
On the general title and those to the third part and the *New Testament*.[13]

147. (254 x 158 mm., enclosing 101 x 76 mm.) A compartment with a cherub's head at top; flowers and fruit in the corners; a mermaid representing Bynneman's sign below (= Device 168).
...
1575 (Nov. 24) by F. Coldock. *The holy byble* (S.T.C. 2110–13a).
On the general title, those to the second part, the third part, the *Apocrypha*, and the *New Testament*.[14]
Variant issues have the names of G. Dewes, L. Harison, W. Norton, and J. Walley as ostensible printers. But on the last preliminary leaf is a colophon giving Richard Jugge's name as printer, with his device (D. 123); and on the last page is H. Bynneman's device (D. 118)[15].

158. (301 x 190 mm., enclosing 102 x 85 mm.) A compartment with the Royal Arms at top between Justice and Mercy (?). A lion and a dragon at foot with C B, the initials of Christopher Barker (= Device 204).[16]
...
1578 by C. Barker. *The bible* (S.T.C. 2123).
On the general title and that to the *New Testament*.[17]
[1583 title to Apocrypha. Page 439 plate blank.]
...
1588 by the Deputies of C. Barker. *The holy bible* (S.T.C. 2149).

13. Ibid., 121.

14. Lion faces top side upper plate. "God save the Queene" bottom plate. New Testament has Rom 1:16 and winged creatures at interior of four corners.

15. McKerrow and Ferguson, *Title-Page Borders*, 125–26.

16. See figure 8.

17. Title John 5:39 in plate.

On the title to the *New Testament*. The lateral portions are printed upside down.

1591 by the Deputies of C. Barker. *The holy bible* (S.T.C. 2156).
On the title to the *New Testament*.

1595 by the Deputies of C. Barker. *The holy bible* (S.T.C. 2167).
On the title to the *New Testament*.[18]

165. (157 x 106.5 mm., enclosing 79 x 48 mm.) A compartment with the Royal Arms at top, Fides and Humilitas at sides; the ensigns of the four evangelists at the corners, and a tiger's head, the crest of Sir F. Walsingham, below (= Device 221).

...

1579 by C. Barker. *The bible* (S.T.C. 2127).
B.M. 347.a.3(i). On the title (C5) to the *Psalter* at the end of the *Book of Common Prayer*.

...

1584 by C. Barker. (*The bible*). (S.T.C. 2142.)
On the titles to the *Psalms* and the *N.T*. Perhaps also on the general title, but no copy containing it seems to be known.[19]

167. (230 x 146 mm., enclosing 130 x 87 mm.) A compartment with female figures bearing plants in vases at sides. At foot a calf's head and two lions scratching masks.

...

1589 by the Deputies of C. Barker. Fulke (W.). *The text of the New Testament* (S.T.C. 2888).[20]

---

18. Lower Press Association 1959, Rom 1: "I am not ashamed of the Gospel." McKerrow and Ferguson, *Title-Page Borders*, 132.

19. McKerrow and Ferguson, *Title-Page Borders*, 136–37.

20. Ibid., 139.

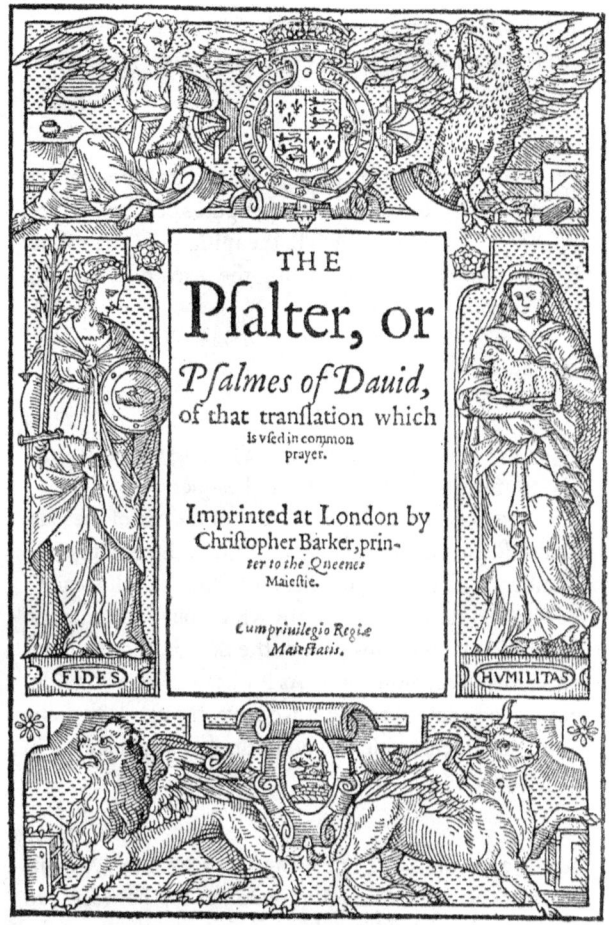

Figure 24: Title to Psalms in Christopher Barker's 1584 Bible, royal coat of arms center top between Fides and Humilitas, ensigns of the four evangelists at corners, crest of Sir Francis Walsingham center bottom.

168. (237 x 151 mm., enclosing 121 x 77 mm.) A compartment with the arms of Elizabeth at top, baskets of fruit at upper corners and bunches of fruit at lower corners.[21]

21. See figure 9.

The Day after Domesday

. . .

1584 by C. Barker. *The holy bible* (S.T.C. 2141).
On the general title and those to the *Apocrypha* and the *New Testament*.[22]

171. (117 x 77 mm., enclosing 70 x 36 mm.) A compartment with the Royal Arms at top; figures of Memoria and Inteligentia at sides; with C B, the initials of Christopher Barker; two cherubs supporting the arms of the Stationer's Company below.[23]
[1579 by C. Barker. *The newe testament*.[24]]
1582 by C. Barker. *The newe testament* (S.T.C. 2883).[25]

199. (313 x 203 mm., enclosing 252 x 143 mm.) A narrow frame border of fruit and arabesques.

This was originally the border of the cut of the Garden of Eden which occurs at the end of the prelims. of a number of editions of the Bishops' Bible in folio, e.g. C. Barker's edition of 1583, from which our reproduction is made. It there forms part of the design, though it appears to be a separate piece. As it was used later as a title-border for a few broadsides we have, though with some hesitation, included it. We do not note its appearance in its original function.[26]

203. (322 x 199 mm., enclosing 114 x 97 mm.) A compartment with the Tetragrammaton at top between two cherubs, a hand holding a book bearing on the cover the words VERBVM DEI MANET IN AETERNV̄: at sides crowned rose and fleur-de-lis and the letters E R crowned: at foot two cherubs.[27]

22. McKerrow and Ferguson, *Title-Page Borders*, 141.
23. See figure 14.
24. Herbert, *Historical Catalogue*, no. 163.
25. McKerrow and Ferguson, *Title-Page Borders*, 144.
26. Ibid., 162.
27. See figure 37. Title page to Psalms but now plate at bottom has Prov 30:6, "Put thou nothing into his words, lest he reprove thee, and thou be found

...

1583 by C. Barker. *The bible* (S.T.C. 2136).
On the general title and that to the *New Testament*.
1585 by C. Barker. *The holy byble* (S.T.C. 2143).
On the general title and that to the *New Testament*.
1588 by the Deputies of C. Barker. *The holy bible* (S.T.C. 2149).
On the general title.
1591 by Deputies of C. Barker. *The holy bible* (S.T.C. 2156).
On the general title.
1595 by the Deputies of C. Barker. *The holy bible* (S.T.C. 2167).
1602 by R. Barker. *The holy bible* (S.T.C. 2188).
B.M. 339.c.5. On the general title and that to the *New Testament*. In another copy (B.M. 340.c.1) of this edition is a different general title containing compartment 231 (our reproduction is taken from it). It is inlaid, so may have been supplied from another edition of the same year, which, however, is not noted in S.T.C. (cf. Sayle, 2574).[28]

259. (124 x 77.5 mm., enclosing 61 x 35 mm.) A compartment with the Tetragrammaton in rayed triangle at top, the four Evangelists at the corners. Female figures at sides. Crowned Royal Arms at foot.
[1606 by R. Barker (72 x 122 mm.). New Testament.[29]]
[1608 by R. Barker. New Testament.[30]]
1613 by R. Barker. *The new testament* (S.T.C. 2912).
The title is partly in red.[31]

Frag. 10 (13 x 53 mm.). Head-piece with triangular pediment.

a liar." New Testament plate quotes Prov 30:5, 6.
    28. McKerrow and Ferguson, *Title-Page Borders*, 163–64.
    29. Herbert, *Historical Catalogue*, no. 288; *STC*, 2905.
    30. Herbert, *Historical Catalogue*, no. 297; *STC*, 2906.
    31. McKerrow and Ferguson, *Title-Page Borders*, 198.

...

1575 Jugge Bible, *New Testament* (S.T.C. 9482).[32]

The final edition of William Fulke's New Testament by A. Matthews in 1633[33] has a title page engraved by William Marchall[34] (260 by 183 millimeters). An evangelist is in each corner, and a priest is on either side.[35]

Other borders are not included in McKerrow and Ferguson. In the 1569 New Testament title, a man and a woman are at the side, and twins are at the bottom as is an oval blank. The 1602 edition has a block with the tribes and the apostles as the 1611 King James Version.[36] In the 1602 Apocrypha title, two women with a coat of arms are at the center, and a lion and dragon are at the bottom. "Testament of Books" is in the center, and the bottom panel is blank.[37]

Illustrations

In addition to these borders, the illustrations within the text, with the exception of one (Herod's feast [pt. 5 xxv recto]), are also enclosed in borders (157 by 119 millimeters exterior and 116 by 77 millimeters interior, but may vary a few millimeters). When an illustration is reused, the border may be different as in Numbers 15:31 of which there are eight varieties reused at random seven to twenty-five times. The printer has unfortunately gotten the compartment upside down at Judges 4:1 and Revelation 14:5.

---

32. Ibid., 218–19.
33. *STC*, 2947.
34. At work 1617–49, see *DNB*.
35. Johnson, *English Title-Pages*, 37.
36. McKerrow and Ferguson, *Title-Page Borders*, 231.
37. Ibid., 158.

Figure 25: Judg 4, woodcut compartment, unfortunately printed upside down (1568).

The pictures themselves are frequently signed "V.S." who is to be identified with Virgil Solis (see figures 6, 9, 10, 11, 15, 16, 19, and 27). These pictures of Solis had earlier been used for a folio Lutheran Bible (1560) published in Frankfurt and in a folio Dutch Bible (1566) published in Cologne.[38] But in addition to Solis, numerous pictures are also signed "S.H.F."

The full page picture of the Tabernacle with the children of Israel camped about it at Exodus 17:21 which contains no border is signed "Cornelius" in the lower left corner (1568, 1572). The picture at Daniel 3:1 is signed "B.S.," and that of Haggai 1:1 is signed "A."

---

38. Hotchkiss and Ryrie, *Formatting the Word of God*.

Figure 26: Exod 17:21, tabernacle with children of Israel camped about, "Cornelius" at lower left (1568).

The woodcuts and most of the compartments of the 1568 edition were not again reproduced in Bishops' Bibles. The 1572 folio has title page borders only for the general title, reproduced from the 1568 edition, and for the New Testament title, which is McKerrow and Ferguson no. 129.[39] An entirely different set of text illustrations, eighteen in number, is used. These pictures are ordinarily composite scenes from stories in the book and occur either at the beginning of the book with Scripture headings above the scenes or occur on title pages:

1. Gen 1:1 (181 by 147 millimeters) — Twelve scenes from Genesis with scripture headings (see figure 21). The interior is formed with a woodcut border (121 by 87 millimeters). The central scene is Adam and the animals in the garden with the Tetragrammaton on the sun (1574).

2. Exod 1:1 (177 by 133 millimeters) — Eight scenes from Exodus with scripture citations (1574).

3. Lev 1:1 (178 by 133 millimeters) — Six scenes from Numbers with scripture headings. Signed on the right bottom between Baalam's donkey's legs "C.T." or "T.K." or "R" (1574).

4. Josh 1:1 (177 by 133 millimeters) — Six scenes from Joshua with scripture headings. Signed "R.B." at the right bottom and "C.T." at the right bottom corner (1574).

5. Judg 1:1 (176 by 133 millimeters) — Nine scenes from Judges with scripture headings. Signed on the stone "R.B."

6. 1 Sam 1:1 (182 by 138 millimeters) — Eleven scenes from Samuel with scripture headings. Signed "C.T." and "R.B." on the lower right (1574).

7. 1 Kgs 1:1 (178 by 134 millimeters) — Twelve scenes from Kings, with scripture headings, dealing with Solomon, Elijah, and Isaiah. Signed at the right bottom corner "R.B." and "C.T."

8. Isa 1:1 (162 by 125 millimeters) — The vision of Isaiah with the Lord on the throne and an angel with tongs and a coal of fire touching the mouth of the prophet (see figure 10). Signed on the coat of a man at the right bottom "T.B." (1574).

---

39. McKerrow and Ferguson, *Title-Page Borders*, 113; *STC*, 2099.

9. Jer 1:1 (178 x 134 millimeters) — Seven scenes from Jeremiah, Ezekiel, and Daniel with scripture headings. Signed "C.T." at the left bottom, and "R.B." on the stone at the center bottom (1574).

10. Title page of Apocrypha — Six scenes from the Apocrypha with texts. Signed on pillar, center bottom "R.B." (1574).

11. Matt 1:1 (79 by 121 millimeters) — The evangelist Matthew seated writing. An angel is at his side, and the Tetragrammaton is on the sun (see figure 20). The picture occupies the left column (1574).

12. Mark 1:1 (78 by 121 millimeters) — The evangelist Mark is seated with a couchant lion at his side. The Tetragrammaton is on the sun. The picture occupies the left column (1574).

Figure 27: Evangelist Mark at opening of his Gospel in 1568 Bible, his symbol the lion, "VS" bottom right.

13. Luke 1:1 (78 by 120 millimeters) — The evangelist Luke is at a table writing on a scroll. A winged ox is reclining at the end of the table (see figure 11). The picture occupies the left column (1574).

14. John 1:1 (77 by 121 millimeters) — The evangelist John on the Isle of Patmos sits on a stump with a book in his hand. An eagle is before him and the Tetragrammaton is on the sun. The picture occupies the left column (1574).

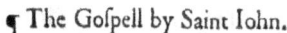

Figure 28: Evangelist John at opening of his Gospel in 1568 Bible, his symbol the eagle.

15. Rom 1:1 (78 by 121 millimeters) — Paul is seated at a table. A large sword is on the floor. Paul presents a letter to a woman, doubtlessly Phoebe, ready for travel (see figure 12). The picture occupies the left column (1574).

16. Jas 1:1 (75 by 120 millimeters) — James with his staff reads in a book. The picture occupies the left column (1574).

17. 1 Pet 1:1 — Peter with a large key and a dip net containing fish reads a book as he walks. The picture occupies the left column (1574).

18. Book of Revelation — Eighteen pictures from Revelation fill the entire page (1574).

The scene at the beginning of Genesis is a bordered scene of the garden of Eden. The border is 121 by 87 millimeters, and around this border are grouped the twelve scenes from Genesis. The whole is 181 by 147 millimeters. Title borders are not used in the remaining pictures. Many are signed "C.T." and "R.G." in the lower part of the pictures. The scene of the garden of Eden in the 1568 edition is a close copy of that in the 1560 Geneva Bible.[40]

The 1574 and 1585 editions reprint the text illustrations of the 1572 edition. Many editions limit themselves to the paradise picture with the compartment while omitting the surrounding pictures. The various quarto editions have no text illustrations.

The Bishops' Bible New Testaments were far less imposing than the folios of the entire Bible. The New Testament, not divided into verses and conjectured to date 1568,[41] has a cut of Paul before 1 Corinthians, Ephesians, and Hebrews. Of the other copies examined, text illustrations are only in two printings and in these only in the book of Revelation. They are DM no. 89[42] and DM no. 99[43] which have twenty illustrations (63 by 42 millimeters) dispersed through the text. In the supplementary material of both of these testaments at the beginning of "A True and Perfect Rendering . . .," there is a scene (43 by 32 millimeters) of the garden of Eden with Eve rising from the side of Adam. The Tetragrammaton is on the sun and animals are about. The picture is signed "A" at the center bottom under a dog.

Title pages are missing from any of the copies in the British and Foreign Bible Society Library. The Testament conjecturally

40. Lovett, *English Bible*, 211.
41. *STC*, 1359 (123) 80.
42. Ibid., 2875, 134.
43. Ibid., 2875a, 136.

dated after 1572[44] has a woodcut border enclosing a circular picture of Edward VI (60 by 55 millimeters). The picture is surrounded by the words: "*Edwardus sextus Die Gloria Anglie Franci et Hibernae Rex. ETC. Aetatis sua XV.*" Testament no. 175[45] has an oval picture (78 by 65 millimeters) as just described, but without the title-page border.

Even less ornate was "The gospel of the fower euangelistes."[46] The border of its title page (167 by 112 millimeters) is a floral design not distinctive enough to describe. The preface to the queen had a decorative letter (51 by 46 millimeters) of floral design and a head under the letter. Otherwise, it is barren of distinctive art.

Illustrations at the beginning of the Gospels, with the exception of Matthew, display the artistic motifs for the evangelists which had become tradition in the gothic art of the Middle Ages. Matthew is symbolized by the angel (see figure 20). Mark is accompanied by the lion (see figure 27), Luke by the ox (see figure 11), and John by the eagle (see figure 28).[47] In 1572, these motifs are from a different block from 1568.

The four editions of the William Fulke New Testament were issued with three sorts of title pages. The editions of 1601 and 1617 use the same block.

1. 1589 (200 by 148 millimeters)—A woman's head is at top center. Maidens with vases of plants are at the bottom corners and an ox at bottom center. The central panel is 130 by 88 millimeters.

2. 1601, 1617 (292 by 185 millimeters)—Two pillars covered with grape vines and clusters of grapes grow out of a pit. "1574" is on the vine above the pot. The top has an oval picture of a sacrificial lamb. The block is signed "N.H." below the lamb picture and "T.C." below the oval. There is a Latin inscription "POSSIDETE ANIMAS VESTRAS."

44. Ibid., 2875, no. 98 (134).
45. Ibid., 2893, 228.
46. Ibid., 2961.
47. Lucas, *Renaissance and Reformation*, 189.

3. 1633 (256 by 180 millimeters)[48]—At the top left, an angel dictates to a man who writes. At the top right, a man has a book and a pen. There is an eagle on the floor at his feet. The center has the manger scene with the adoration of the babe of Bethlehem. On the left side is an open book and on the right an angel standing on a table. Abandoned weapons are on the ground, and a man flees the majesty of the angel. At the center left side is a popish figure with beads and the words "*Hinc Zizania.*" At the right side is an Elizabethan preacher with a Bible and the words: "*Verbum Dei Hinc semen Bonum.*" At the right bottom, a man writes with the ox under his feet, while at the bottom left, another writes with the lion under his feet. At the bottom center are two men with "*Novum Testamentum*" between them. The engraving is signed in small script at the right bottom: "*Wille Marshall Scuplsit*" (William Marchall).[49]

In the 1572 edition, the map of Palestine covering a full opening (two pages) at Josh 21 has a plate to the lower right, "Graven by Hvmfray Cole, goldsmith, a Englishman born in ye north and pertayning to ye Mint in the Tower, 1572."[50] There is the coat of arms of Lord Burghley at the right bottom as previously mentioned.

The map of the Holy Land in the 1574 edition appears to be the same used in Coverdale's Bible of 1535, cut on wood but not signed.[51]

Initial Letters

Many of the initial letters were suggested by mythology. The 1572 edition had as many as 114 varieties, some of which were made by Arnold Nicolai.[52] The mammoth task required to describe all of these cannot be undertaken here. However, a few of the initials

---

48. 260 by 183 millimeters. Johnson, *English Title-Pages*, 37.
49. Ibid.
50. Corbett and Norton, *Engraving in England*, 80.
51. Ames, *Typographical Antiquities*, 4:259.
52. Clair, *History of Printing*, 289.

are worthy of special notice since they are identifiable scenes from mythology.

1. The letter "T" illustrated with Neptune taming the sea horses (55 by 57 millimeters). Two blocks were used, one containing "M.C." superimposed on the scene (1568—Exod 1:1, Matt 1:1; 1572—Exod 1:1, 2 Esd 1:1, Mic 1:1, Nah 1:1; 1602—Matt 1:1) and the other without it (1568, 1572—Deut 1:1, Prov 1:1, Jonah 1:1, Hab 1:1, Zeph 1:1, Matt 1:1, Mark 1:1, Acts 1:1). The latter was also used in the 1611 King James Version at Matt 1:1 and Rev 1:1 (see figure 4).

2. The letter "P" decorated with scene of Daphne becoming a laurel tree (1568, 1572—2 Cor 1:1, Eph 1:1, Phil 1:1, 1 Thess 1:1, Titus 1:1, Phlm 1:1, 1 Pet 1:1; 1611 [King James Version]—Rom 1:1; 1692—Letter "I" with scene of Daphne, Gen 1:1).

3. The Letter "T" decorated with scene in which Zeus with trident sits in court. Cupid is before him as well as a woman with bare breasts (1572—1 Sam 1:1, 1 John 1:1, Rev 1:1; 1574—Preface to New Testament).

4. The letter "G" decorated with scene of Leda and the swan. It is this letter that has given the name "The Leda Bible" to this edition (1572—Heb 1:1).

5. The letter "F" decorated with the huntsman who shoots his daughter instead of a stag (1568—Eph 3:3).

6. The letter "A" with two women, one standing and one seated (56 by 56 millimeters). The block is signed "C" on the pillar top center near the standing woman (1568—Lev 1:1, Num 1:1, 1 Chr 1:1, 2 Chr 1:1, Lam 1:1, Sir 1:1, Bar 1:1, 1 Macc 1:1. See figure 7).

Some of the letters were used in the following year (1569) in an edition of Grafton's *Chronicle* published by Henry Denbon.[53]

---

53. Cotton, *Editions of the Bible*, 299.

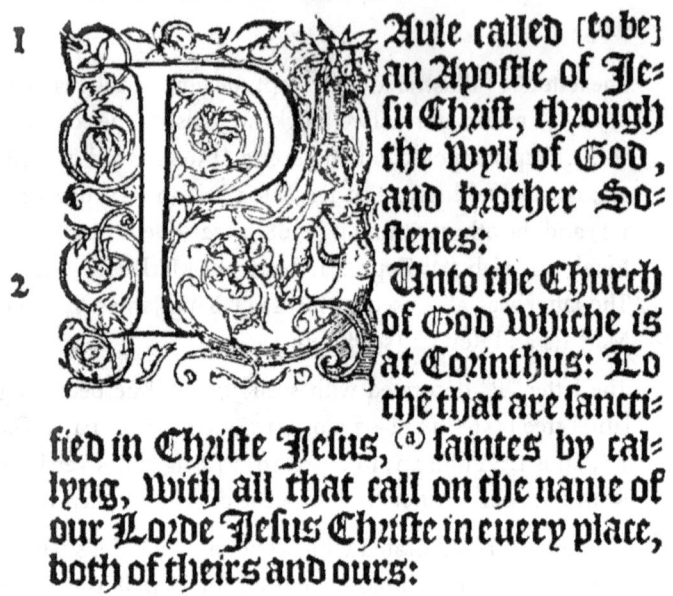

Figure 29: Initial letter "P," Daphne becoming a laurel tree, at 1 Cor 1:1 (1568).

In the 1574 edition title to the third part of the Bible (163 by 123 millimeters), there is a seraph preparing to go to war. His horse is being held, and a dog is in the center foreground.

Coats of Arms

Numerous very fine coats of arms were in various editions. At Cranmer's preface (1568), the initial "C" has Cranmer's arms impaled with those of the see of Canterbury. On the right hand of the arms to the back of the letter is the letter "T" (see figure 2).

The arms of Matthew Parker are at the genealogy of Christ from Adam (1568). The initial "T" has the archbishop's paternal arms, impaled with that of Christchurch, Canterbury, with the initials "M.P." on each side and the date 1568 at the bottom. The cross's staff with its head in the place of the crest runs through the stem of the "T." The encircling motto reads "MUNDUS TRANSIT ET CONCVPISCENTIA EIVS" (see figure 3). For the Preface to Bible (1568), the initial "O" has Parker's paternal coat of arms with the motto around it and "M.P." on each side. The cross's staff goes through the arms and the top of it appears. In the 1569 edition at Genesis 1:1, the letter "I" is set within Parker's arms, impaled by those of the see of Canterbury. The 1573 edition has Parker's arms at Genesis 1:1. A map of the Holy Land in the 1574 edition has Parker's arms impaled with those of the deanery instead of the archbishopric of Canterbury.

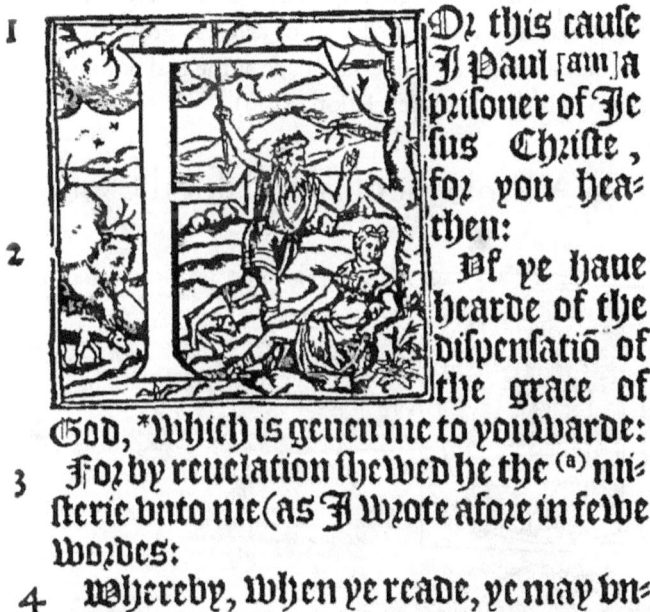

Figure 30: Initial letter "F," huntsman who shoots his daughter, at Eph 3:3 (1568).

111

The arms of Leicester appear at Joshua 1:1 (1569) with the letter "A" and the motto "DRAIT ET LOYAL." The arms of Leicester also appear in the initial of Joshua in the 1572 edition and at Joshua 1:1 in the 1573 edition.

William Cecil's coat of arms is at the title page of the book of Psalms with the letter "B" (Lord Burghley) and the motto "*Cor unum via umb*" (1569). The initial "D" is on the verso of the title page of Psalms in the 1572 edition. Also in the 1572 edition, the map of Palestine has a coat of arms of Lord Burghley at the right bottom with lions and "*cor vnvm via vna.*"

A coat of arms of the Earl of Bedford is with the "T" (2 3/4 by 3 3/8 inches) at the beginning of the book of Jeremiah (1572).[54] There is also an unidentified coat of arms at Proverbs 1:1 and a regal coat of arms filling one-half page at the end of John's Gospel and also of the book of Revelation (1579).

Figure 31: Verso to Ps 1 in 1568 Bible, coat of arms of William Cecil, first Baron Burghley.

---

54. Lovett, *English Bible*, 222.

Conclusion

The art work of the first edition of the Bishops' Bible is distinctive, from the title page with the copperplate engraved portrait of Queen Elizabeth, to the large decorative first letters that begin each book, to the traditional symbols depicting the four Gospel writers. The total number of engravings, woodcuts, and maps is 143. There are a total of 124 woodcut borders for biblical scenes at their relevant places, many of these carrying the initial of the carver.[55]

The art work was not constant in later editions. The 1569 quarto did not have the woodcuts. The 1572 edition had only thirty illustrations.

---

55. Cf. Aston, "*Bishops' Bible* Illustrations," 267–85; Clair, "Bishops' Bible," 287–90.

7

"A New Translation . . . to Rectify the Former"

Hugh Broughton

AMONG THE MOST VOCAL agitators urging Archbishop Whitgift for a further revision of Scriptures was Hugh Broughton (1549–1612), a Cambridge-trained rabbinical scholar who had entered Magdalene College in 1569 and for a period distinguished himself in London as a preacher of Puritan sentiment. In polity, however, Broughton held to the episcopacy as apostolic.

Though eccentric and egotistical, Broughton was doubtless a man of much ability, was adored by his own pupils, but was of caustic tongue and was sharp with others. One of his opponents said of him, "and therefore writing about the descent into Hell, hath inflamed his own tongue with the fire of hell . . ."[1] Thomas Fuller says, "His sermons were generally on subjects rather for curiosity than edification."[2] Broughton, perhaps fearing clerical censure, traveled on the continent after 1589 and was a disputant against both Catholicism and the Jews, as well as against Beza. He later bore the brunt of satire of Ben Jonson in "Volpone" (2.2.128) and in "The Alchemist" (2.2.488–89; 4.5.478–79).[3]

In a letter of June 21, 1593, to William Cecil, Broughton claimed "That sundry Lords, and among them some Bishops, and

---

1. STC, 3864, 18.
2. Fuller, *Worthies of England*, 3:503.
3. *DNB*, 2:1387–1370.

others inferior of all sorts, had requested or wished him to bestow his long studies in Hebrew and Greek writers upon some clearing of the Bible's translation. That they judged rightly, that amended it must be." He declined to be specific in advance of publication about the needed improvements "that it [the Bible] less be disgraced which they then used" but "all of knowledge and conscience would grant, that bettered much it might be." Broughton further claimed earlier indirect and unofficial encouragement from the queen and that Walsingham had intended to take his part but had been too busy to do so. Broughton urged Cecil to take initiative and appoint six scholars (of whom it goes without saying Broughton would be one) to the task. He envisioned the use of notes, maps, and tables of chronicles in the edition.[4]

Figure 32: Map, Holy Land places mentioned in the four evangelists, verso to title page of New Testament (1568).

4. Strype, *Life and Acts of John Whitgift*, 2:4:225–26.

The Day after Domesday

In 1597 at Middleburgh, Broughton issued "An Epistle to the learned nobilitie of England, touching translating the Bible from the Original."[5] Broughton insisted that a "translator must avoid all lyes" under which category he listed items in the Bishops' translation such as Genesis 10:21 which made Japheth younger than Shem (as Tyndale, Coverdale, and the Great Bible). Broughton argued for "Shem the Elder" (King James Version). In Genesis 49:5, 15, the translation read "prophecy" (as Tyndale and Coverdale, but the Great Bible had "divine and prophecy") whereas Broughton preferred "search thoroughly." In Exodus 12:40, the Bishops' read "dwelling" and "dwelt" rather than "peregrination" and "sojourned."[6] In Hebrews 2:1, Broughton favored "lest we flow" rather than "lest we let them slip" (as the Great Bible).[7] Broughton complained that Whitgift had put a halt to the work on Daniel which Broughton had prepared: "And I dare to defend his grace for that translation: that it was better than the usual in the church."[8]

On June 11, 1597, in another letter to Cecil, Broughton further blamed Whitgift for hindering "a new translation . . . to rectify the former." He spoke of his own treatise as "written to all the realm for the true Bible." He claimed to have shown Whitgift one error, "the highest flat atheism," but said "the Archbishop is within a hairbreath to shame his nation for ever, in a matter the highest for religion." Broughton insisted that England needed a Bible "by a linguist."[9] In the same year in a letter to the queen, Broughton alluded to the fact that he was about to "*open* the *Bible* to her Majesty" by his new translation of it out of the Hebrew.[10]

Broughton held to the absolute incorruptness of the text of both Testaments, including the Hebrew vowel points. He argued that both the *kethibh* and the *qere* are "of God and of equal authority." He argued that one error in a translation corrupted the

---

5. *STC*, 3862.
6. Ibid., 3862, 12, 15, 20.
7. Ibid., 3862, 53.
8. Ibid., 3862, 34–35.
9. Strype, *Life and Acts of John Whitgift*, 2:4:355–57.
10. Ibid., 2:4:389.

"A New Translation... to Rectify the Former"

whole.[11] Broughton advocated consistency in the translation of words and the use of popular speech.[12]

Blessed is the man that walketh not in the counsell of the ungodly: nor standeth in the way of sinners, nor sitteth in the seate of the scornefull.

But his delight [is] in the lawe of God: and in [God] his lawe exerciseth himselfe day and night.

And he shalbe lyke a tree planted "by the waters syde, that bryngeth foorth her fruite in due season: and whose leafe wythereth not, for whatsoeuer he doth (a) it shall prosper.

[As for] the ungodly [it is] not so [with them:] but they [are] like the chaffe which the winde scattereth abrode.

Therefore the ungodly shall not [be able to] "stande in the iudgement: neither the sinners in the congregation of the righteous.

For God (b) knoweth the way of the righteous: and the way of the ungodly shall perishe.

Figure 33: Opening of Psalms in 1568 Bible, decorative "B," portrait of William Cecil, later Lord Burghley.

Broughton was not beyond giving the Bishops' Bible credit in selected places. He favored its retention of the doxology at the end of the Lord's Prayer (Matt 6:15), which the Rheims New Testament, the communion book, and some other authorities known to him omitted.[13] He approved its implication that Abraham was born when his father was age 130 rather than at 75.[14]

On the other hand, his attack on the Bishops' Bible included its notes. Broughton insisted that Matthew Parker "suffered bad

---

11. Ibid., 2:4:221–22; cf. *STC*, 386, 21.
12. *STC*, 3862, 3–4.
13. Ibid., 3867, 21.
14. Ibid., 3844, 80.

notes to bring in error, a thousand at once, to make all the credit of Moses and the prophets worth nothing."[15]

Broughton had long standing conflicts with John Reynolds of Oxford that go back at least to 1588 when Reynolds attacked Broughton's "A Concent of Scripture." Despite Broughton's hinting, pleading, and near blackmail in his threats to give his work to other countries if neglected, it is not surprising he was bypassed in the selection of the committees for preparing the new Bible under King James.

Meanwhile, Broughton could solace himself by preparing his own version of the prophets and Job, the latter of which was issued in 1610.[16] Broughton had written the king in August 1604 commending him for the undertaking of the new translation and had laid out a method of procedure which included that a qualified one (doubtless Broughton himself) should go over the whole.[17] He wrote "That all this while the Bishops were unwilling that their traps and pitfalls should be taken away, until his Majesty forced them to it."[18]

Still failing to gain the position he sought, he became even more vehement in his criticisms of the Bishops' Bible. In 1604, he issued "an Advertisement of Corruption in our Handling of Religion,"[19] in which he voiced objection to "silk" for the material of the ephod and objected to the names chosen for the precious stones in the Old Testament.[20] Offensive also was Acts 13:19, "about the space of 450 years," for which he advocated, "after a sort 450 yeeres," and he said of it, "So our Bishops' Bible might as well give place to the Alkoran pestered with lyes."[21] In 1 Kings 15:33, he argued for "kingdom" rather than "reign" and commented:

---

15. Strype, *Life and Acts of John Whitgift*, 2:4:221.
16. STC, 3868.
17. Strype, *Life and Acts of John Whitgift*, 2:4:528–29.
18. Ibid., 2:4:527–28.
19. Another edition is dated 1605; STC, 3844.
20. STC, 3844, 86–87.
21. Ibid., 3844, 63.

"A New Translation... to Rectify the Former"

Our Bishops' translation that Machmadistes may by our Divinity look for their false Prophet to revive, as did Bassa by our Bible. When Gentlemen find such matters in our Bibles they see no hope of knowledge, and some have turned to deny God to be the auctor of it.[22]

It was, however, the table preceding the New Testament that particularly drew Broughton's wrath. Of it he said, "the cockles of the Sea shores and the leaves of a Forest, and the granes of the Popy, may as well be numbered as the grosse errours of this Table, disgracing the ground of our own hope."[23]

In 1609, Broughton issued "Principal positions for groundes of the holy bible," one part of which is "A short oration of the Bible's Translation," in which more of his problem passages and his choice of renderings were set out. Still putting himself forth as one qualified for the task, he said:

> None should bear away in translating but the able to shew what Thalmudiques have said to every word of the Law: and the able to discerne the foure varieties of the Apostles Greeke; how much in the Heathen sort, how much after the 72, what the Apostles better translate and what space as did Thalmudiques.[24]

But it was all in vain. The new translation went forth without Broughton and in spite of him.

When the Bible finally appeared in 1611, Broughton was its chief critic also:

> The late Bible, Right Worshipful, was sent to me to censure: which bred in me a sadness that will greeve me while I breath[e]. It is so ill done. Tell his Maiest that I had rather be rent in pieces with wild horses, then any such translation by my consent should bee urged upon poore Churches.[25]

---

22. Ibid., 3844.
23. Ibid., 3844, 47.
24. Ibid., 3880.
25. Broughton, *Censure of the Late Translation*, 1; STC, 3847.

The Making of the King James

John Reynolds gave further voice to the dissatisfaction of the Puritans with the Scriptures in the Prayer Book at the second day of the Hampton Court Conference, January 15, 1604.

> He moued his Maiestie, that there might bee a newe *translation* of the *Bible*, because, those which were allowed in the raignes of *Henrie* the eight, and *Edward* the sixt, were corrupt and not aunswerable to the truth of the Originall.[26]

No specific mention of the Bishops' Bible was made. The cases of corruption cited by Reynolds—"bordereth" (Gal 4:23), "they were not obedient" (Ps 150:28), and "Phinees ... prayed" (Ps 106:30)—are aimed at the Great Bible, but appeared in later Bishops' Bibles as well since the Bishops' Psalms were not again printed after 1585. The first of these examples had remained unchanged from Tyndale. The second read in the 1572 Bishops' Bible "they went not from his wordes" whereas Reynolds favored "not disobedient." The third read "executed justice" but Reynolds wished "executed judgement." The cases are classed by Barlow as "trivial, and old, and already in print, often aunswered."[27]

James I was favorable toward an effort for "one uniform translation" to which "no marginal notes should be added." The rules were drawn up, and rule one instructed: "The ordinary Bible read in the Church, commonly called the *Bishops' Bible*, to be followed, and as little altered as the Truth of the original will permit." Rule fourteen further provided: "These translations to be used when they agree better with the Text than the *Bishops' Bible*: Tindoll's [sic], Matthews, Coverdale's, Whitchurch's, Geneva."[28]

To the Synod of Dort, it was reported:

---

26. Barlow, *Summe and Substance of the Conference*, 45; cf. "The Translators to the Reader," in Pollard, *Records of the English Bible*, 46.

27. Barlow, *Summe and Substance of the Conference*, 46.

28. Pollard, *Records of the English Bible*, 53–54.

"A New Translation... to Rectify the Former"

In the first place caution was given that an entirely new version was not to be furnished, but an old version, long received by the Church, to be purged from all blemishes and faults; to this end there was to be no departure from the ancient translation, unless the truth of the original text or emphasis demanded.[29]

No open attack was made by the revisers on the earlier Bishops' effort. In the "Translators to the Reader," they say:

> We are so farre off from condemning any of their labours that traueiled before vs in this kinde, either in this land or beyond sea, either in King *Henries* time, or King *Edwards* (if there were any translation, or correction of a translation in his time) or Queene *Elizabeths* of euer-renoumed memorie, that we acknowledge them to haue beene raised vp of God, for the building and furnishing of his Church, and that they deserue to be had of vs and of posteritie in euerlasting remembrance.[30]

They continue:

> Wee neuer thought from the beginning, that we should neede to make a New Translation, nor yet to make of a bad one a good one . . . but to make a good one better, or out of many good ones, one principall good one, not iustly to be excepted against; that hath bene our indeauour, that our marke.[31]

John Selden (1584–1654), the jurist, said:

> The *English* Translation of the Bible is the best Translation in the World, and renders the Sense of the Original best, taking in for the *English* Translation the Bishops' Bible as well as King *James*'.[32]

The first printing of the King James Version in 1611 carried the words "Appointed to be read in the Churches," but the "second

---

29. Ibid., 339.
30. Ibid., 359.
31. Ibid., 369.
32. Selden, *Table-Talk*, 5.

folio, 1611; 8vo, 1612; folio, 1613; 4to, 1613; 8vo, 1613; Blackletter 4to, 1613; N.T. 12mo, 1611; and N.T. 4to, 1616," do not have these words.[33] No official decree was made. The articles of visitation of the period are not uniform. Davidson found thirteen between 1512 and 1561 asking for "A Bible of the last translation" and twelve for only "A Bible of the largest Volume."[34]

The gradual displacing of the Bishops' Bible by the Authorized Version is to be seen in purchase and in presentments. In Oxfordshire, the wardens of Cropredy (1616) said:

> We have all things decent in the article mentioned having that our byble in certen leaves are rent. We stay the provydinge of a new, for that we understand there is appointed by the King's Authorities a new shortly to be impressed for the whole realm, when we shal be willinge to provide of that sorte.[35]

On the other hand, those of Horley answer in 1619: "We have an English bible of the largest volume, but not that which was lately set forth by his maiestyes authority."[36]

Wardens of Walton, Yorkshire, in 1613 are charged: "They want a bible of the largest volume" and are ordered to provide one.[37] Wardens of Bishopthorpe, Yorkshire, are charged in 1651: "They want a Bible of the new translation."[38]

In 1612, Wimborne paid fifty-six shillings "for the church Bible."[39] Saint Mary's Reading, Berkshire, disposed of their Bible in 1612–14 with an entry: "for the ould byble by Mr Will's Iremonger seven shillings."[40] Saint Mary Devizes in 1614 paid "Sam Clark for a new Bible of the new Translation" forty shillings.[41] In 1620,

33. Davidson, "Authorisation of the English Bible," 441.
34. Ibid., 442.
35. Peyton, *Churchwardens' Presentments*, 244.
36. Ibid., 238.
37. Skaife, "Extracts from the Visitation," 238.
38. Ibid., 229.
39. Cox, *Churchwardens' Accounts*, 118.
40. Garry and Garry, *Churchwardens' Accounts*, 120.
41. Cox, *Churchwardens' Accounts*, 118.

"A New Translation... to Rectify the Former"

Great Wigston purchased a new Bible for forty shillings and sold the old one for ten.[42] Saint Maratin's Leicester paid forty shillings in 1620–21.[43] Bewley, Worcestershire, paid fifty-five shillings "for the newe bible for the chappell and caridge of him from London."[44] Saint Nicholas Strood enters under "Money Layd owte," "for a new church bible of the last translation, thirty-two shillings."[45]

The Bishops' Bible did not disappear either from church or private use immediately. New Testament printings continued until 1618, and Fulke's work was reprinted in 1633. Sermons preached by Bishop Andrews in 1614, Bishop Buchner of Rochester in 1626, and Dr. Gryffith Williams in 1624 take their texts from the Bishops' Bible.[46] Bishop Buckridge's funeral sermon for Bishop Andrews took its text from the Bishops' Bible.[47] A British Museum copy of the 1575 folio (3036.33.6) contains anonymous manuscript notes in which the whole is divided in three-chapters-a-day readings beginning January 1, 1625. The reader skips the Apocrypha and arrives at 1 John at December 31.

Copies of Bishops' Bibles continued to be used for family birth records long after there is any reason to suppose they were read. The Folger Library copy of the 1573 edition has family records of 1691–1701. The Library of Congress copy of the 1569 Bible records the birth of Isaac Matthews, May 16, Friday, at four in the morning, 1697, and of a person named Elizabeth, May 17, 1731.

The final stage in the life of the Bishops' Bible is its role as an antiquarian item. When the Bagster's *Hexapla* of the New Testament was prepared in 1841, the Bishops' Bible was omitted from the versions printed. Rounds, on the other hand, printed selected verses from the Old Testament but likewise did not use the Bishops' in the New Testament. It was not until the issuing of *The New Testament Octapla* (1962) that the Bishops' version was made

---

42. Plomer, *Churchwardens' Accounts*, 119.
43. North, *Accounts of the Church Wardens*, 162.
44. Bruton, *History of Bewdley*, xxvii.
45. Plomer, *Churchwardens' Accounts*, 119.
46. Davidson, "Authorisation of the English Bible," 441–42.
47. Westcott, *General View of the History*, 107, note 1.

generally available for textual comparison. The *Octapla* prints the 1602 text rather than the text of the first edition. *The Genesis Octapla* (1965) prints the Bishops' Genesis.

Figure 34: Map, location of Garden of Eden, Gen 2 (1568).

In 1821, the Bodleian Library paid sixteen pounds, ten shillings, for a first edition Bishops' Bible. Offor's copy, when sold, brought forty-one pounds, and Lea Wilson's brought sixteen pounds, ten shillings.[48]

---

48. MacRay, *Bodleian Library*, 308.

Conclusion

THE BISHOPS' BIBLE IS essentially a phenomenon of the Elizabethan Age. It was, except for the several printings of the New Testament after James I came to the throne, composed and published in its completeness (1568–1602) only during the thirty-four years of Elizabeth's reign.

After Queen Mary Tudor died (November 17, 1559), Anglicans came from their places of hiding; those on the continent hurried home hoping to fill church appointments. Matthew Parker was consecrated as archbishop of Canterbury.

Selected exiles, remaining in Geneva, completed the Geneva Bible in 1560. The Epistle at its beginning read: "To the Moste Vertvovs and Noble Qvene Elisabet, Qvene of England, France and Ireland, &c." However, no public acknowledgement of the version on her part was ever made. On January 8, 1561, Thomas Bodley was granted for seven years the exclusive privilege of printing it in England;[1] however, he did not exercise the right until 1576.

No Bibles had been printed in England during the five years of Mary's reign. Elizabeth's injunction ordered that the whole Bible "of the largest volume"[2] be provided. The Great Bible would have been the one available. On the continent, there were printings of the Geneva Bible. Parker remarked to Elizabeth of notes

---

1. Pollard, *Records of the English Bible*, 185–86.
2. Eadie, *English Bible*, 2:62–63.

in translations "that might have ben also well spared,"³ suggesting that a new Bible would be desirable.

Cranmer, earlier writing to Cromwell on August 5, 1537, projected that the bishops would not set forth a better Bible than Matthew's (which he was commending) "till a day after domesday."⁴

Thirty years later, such an effort was drawing near. Richard Cox, bishop of Ely, on January 9, 1561, proposed to William Cecil, secretary to Elizabeth, the need of a new translation.⁵

Following a pattern that Cranmer had unsuccessfully attempted in 1542,⁶ Parker distributed parcels of Scripture to various reviewers. Parker explained to Elizabeth, when the whole was completed, that the Bible used in the churches (the Great Bible) was retained except where it differed from Hebrew and Greek originals. Sections and divisions were used in the text as Pagnine and Münster. "No bitter notis" were to be made "or yet to set downe any determinacion in places of controversie." Sections not to be publicly read, such as genealogies, were to be marked. All words in the translation giving offense in lightness or obscenity were to be replaced with more convenient terms and phrases. The printer had used his thickest paper in the New Testament "bicause yt shalbe most occupied."⁷ Richard Cox in a letter to Parker suggested that inkhorn terms (i.e., ostentatiously learned) were to be avoided.⁸

John Eadie estimated that the revision began about 1563 and that about four years were spent in the project.⁹ Letters to Parker acknowledging receipt of a section or return of a section do survive. With the review well under way, Parker and Grendal petitioned the queen to extend Bodley's privilege of printing the Geneva Bible for twelve years.¹⁰

3. Pollard, *Records of the English Bible*, 295.
4. Ibid., 215.
5. Ibid., 287.
6. Ibid., 274.
7. Ibid., 297–98.
8. Ibid., 291.
9. Eadie, *English Bible*, 2:73.
10. Pollard, *Records of the English Bible*, 286.

Conclusion

Parker wrote September 22, 1568, to Cecil announcing the completion of the project except for some "ornamentes,"[11] and then a later letter of October 5 explained that for health reasons Parker could not present his work to the queen. He asked Cecil to make the presentation and asked that a printing privilege be granted to Richard Jugge to safeguard his investment in the book.

The Bible carried the queen's picture on its title page. It had no dedication; it did not during Parker's life carry the phrase "Appointed to be read in churches." The Great Bible, printed in 1568, did have these words. Not until 1577 did the Bishops' Bible carry "Set forth by authority," which meant by Episcopal authority, not by royal authority either of queen or Parliament.

Revisers

The Bible was a church product rather than one of the language scholars of the day. Two lists of revisers, that are not in complete agreement, are extant—one in Parker's letter to Elizabeth and the other the initials in the printed book. At least a dozen were bishops,[12] and others became bishops later. One was a dean,[13] and two were prebendaries.[14] All were Anglicans. Biographical summaries of most are in the *Dictionary of National Biography*, in Heaton's *The Puritan Bible*,[15] and some in Lewis Lupton.[16] They worked independently; there were no face-to-face meetings and discussions by the participants.

---

11. Ibid., 291–92.
12. William Alley, Richard Davies, Edwyn Sandys, Robert Horne, Nicholas Bullingham, Edmund Scambler, Thomas Cole, Edmund Grindel, William Barlow, John Parkhurst, Richard Cox, Gabriel Goodman, and Hugh Jones.
13. Gabriel Goodman.
14. Andrew Pierson and Andrew Perne.
15. Heaton, *Puritan Bible*, 158–230.
16. Lupton, *Geneva Bible*, 22:61–110.

Description

The Bishops' Bible (number six in the sequence of printed English Bibles),[17] like its predecessors, had extensive study materials of twenty-four folio pages inserted before the text. Included was Parker's preface in Roman type and Cranmer's prologue in black letter. There was a table of genealogy from Adam to Christ. Within the text at Leviticus 18:10 was a table listing unlawful kinships for marriage. The book of Psalms had the prologue of Saint Basil on the Psalms. Parker also had a preface before the New Testament. Following the book of Revelation was "A table to Find the Epistles and Gospels read in the Church of England."

The Bishops' Bible was printed in black letter type with the headings in Roman type. Like in its predecessors from Coverdale on, the twelve books of the Apocrypha were included between the Old Testament and New Testament. The artwork of the first edition is distinctive and elegant.

Revision

The second edition, a quarto of 1569, had been extensively revised. Between the issuing of the second and third editions of this Bible, Elizabeth was excommunicated by Pope Pius V in Rome on February 26, 1570. A convocation of Canterbury in 1571 ordered the house of every bishop as well as churches to have a Bible. The third edition, that of 1572, printed in black letter, had revision in both the Old Testament and New Testament but did not make use of the correction of 1569. The Great Bible Psalms (the Prayer Book Psalms) were printed in parallel columns with the Bishops' Psalms. All later printings of the Bishops' Bible, except the 1585 edition which had the Bishops' Psalms, carried these Great Bible Psalms rather than the Bishops'.

---

17. Coverdale's, 1535; Matthew's, 1537; Taverner's, 1539; the Great Bible, 1539; the Geneva, 1560; and the Bishops', 1568.

Conclusion

Collations of sections of the Bishops' Bible with the Great Bible and the Geneva Bible have been done by Eadie,[18] Edgar,[19] Mombert,[20] Moulton,[21] Westcott,[22] and Lupton.[23]

Translators have had trouble with what the horse should say in Job 39:25. The Bishops' has, "He sayeth among the trumpets, Ha, Ha." Colossians 2:13 reads, "dead to sin and to the uncircumcision of your flesh," which would be thought a printer's error were not the preposition "to" repeated. Most awkward is, "prepare your pre-promised benefice, that it might be ready as a benefice and not an extortion" (2 Cor 9:5).

Like all books of its time, the Bishops' had its printing errors. The 1572 edition of the New Testament at Ephesians 4:14 has "wilderness [for 'wileness'] of Men." All Bishops' printings that have the Great Bible Psalms repeat its error: "The righteous shall be punished" (Ps 37:28). The Prayer Book was not corrected until 1661.

The Bishops' reverted from "The foole hath sayd in his heart, there is no god" to Coverdale's and Matthew's, "The foolish bodies say in their hert, 'Tush, there is no God'" (Ps 14:1).

The Bishops' had many fewer notes than did the Geneva. Those included cover alternate readings, references to similar passages, and comments explanatory of the text. An extensive indebtedness to Geneva has been identified. Notes are not identical in all editions. A 1577 quarto reads at Genesis 1:14, "These lights were not made to serue astronomers phantasies, but for signes in natural thynges, and tokens of gods mercy or wrath."

A note to Psalm 45:9 reads, "Ophir is thought to be the Llande in the west coast, of late founde by Christopher Columbo; from whence at this day is brought most fine gold."

---

18. Eadie, *English Bible*.
19. Edgar, *Bibles of England*.
20. Mombert, *English Versions of the Bible*.
21. Moulton, *History of the English Bible*.
22. Westcott, *General View of the History*.
23. Lupton, *Geneva Bible*, 22:50–95.

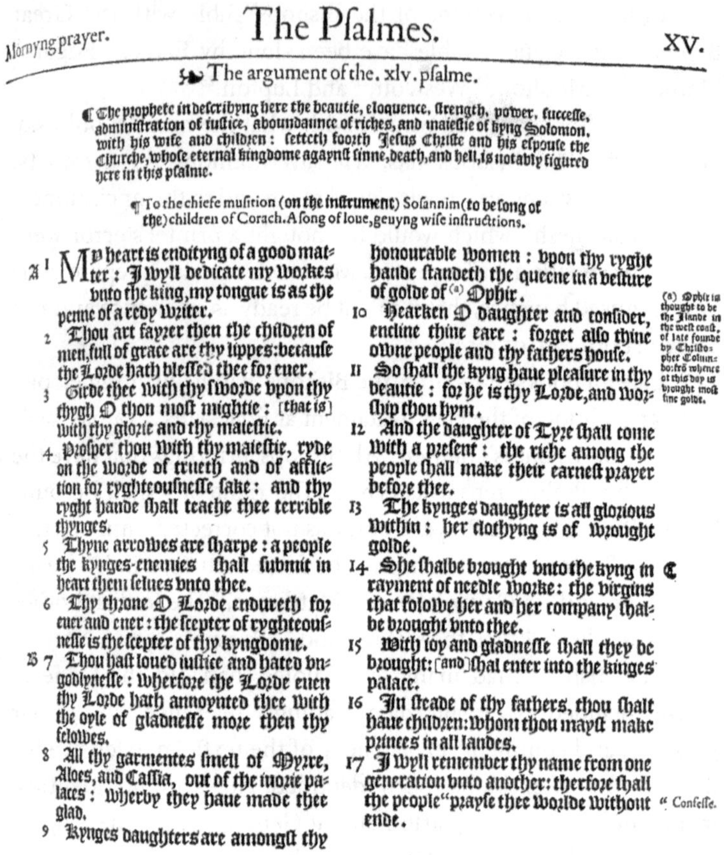
Mornyng prayer. The Psalmes. XV.

The argument of the. xlv. psalme.

The prophete in describyng here the beautie, eloquence, strength, power, successe, administration of iustice, aboundaunce of riches, and maiestie of kyng Solomon, with his wife and children: setteth foorth Jesus Christe and his espouse the Churche, whose eternal kingdome agaynst sinne, death, and hell, is notably figured here in this psalme.

¶ To the chiefe musition (on the instrument) Sosannim (to be song of the) children of Corach. A song of loue, geuyng wise instructions.

A 1 My heart is endityng of a good matter: I wyll dedicate my workes
vnto the king, my tongue is as the
penne of a redy writer.
2 Thou art fayrer then the children of
men, full of grace are thy lippes: because
the Lorde hath blessed thee for euer.
3 Girde thee with thy sworde vpon thy
thygh O thou most mightie: [that is]
with thy glorie and thy maiestie.
4 Prosper thou with thy maiestie, ryde
on the worde of trueth and of afflic-
tion for ryghteousnesse sake: and thy
ryght hande shall teache thee terrible
thynges.
5 Thyne arrowes are sharpe: a people
the kynges-enemies shall submit in
heart them selues vnto thee.
6 Thy throne O Lorde endureth for
euer and euer: the scepter of ryghteousnesse is the scepter of thy kyngdome.
B 7 Thou hast loued iustice and hated vn-
godlynesse: wherfore the Lorde euen
thy Lorde hath annoynted thee with
the oyle of gladnesse more then thy
felowes.
8 All thy garmentes smell of Myrre,
Aloes, and Cassia, out of the iuorie pa-
laces: wherby they haue made thee
glad.
9 Kynges daughters are amongst thy
honourable women: vpon thy ryght
hande standeth the queene in a vesture
of golde of (a) Ophir.
10 Hearken O daughter and consider,
encline thine eare: forget also thine
owne people and thy fathers house.
11 So shall the kyng haue pleasure in thy
beautie: for he is thy Lorde, and worship thou hym.
12 And the daughter of Tyre shall come
with a present: the riche among the
people shall make their earnest prayer
before thee.
13 The kynges daughter is all glorious
within: her clothyng is of wrought
golde.
14 She shalbe brought vnto the kyng in C
rayment of needle worke: the virgins
that folowe her and her company shalbe brought vnto thee.
15 With ioy and gladnesse shall they be
brought: [and] shal enter into the kinges
palace.
16 In steade of thy fathers, thou shalt
haue children: whom thou mayst make
princes in all landes.
17 I wyll remember thy name from one
generation vnto another: therfore shall
the people " prayse thee worlde without
ende.

(a) Ophir is thought to be the Ilande in the west coast, of late founde by Christopher Columbo: fro whence at this day is brought most fine golde.

" Confesse.

Figure 35: Note to Ps 45:9, referring to Christopher Columbus (1568).

A note about the wise men at Matthew 2:12 reads, "Promises ought not to be kept where God's honour and the preaching of the truth is hindered, the wise men, notwithstanding their promise made unto Herod, returned home into their owne countries by another way."

Conclusion

Printers

The first editions of the Bishops' Bible were issued by Richard Jugge, whose shop was at the north door of Saint Paul's churchyard, London. His mark was that of the pelican feeding her young. Jugge, after a printing career of thirty years, died in 1577; a quarto edition of that year, at the end of the New Testament, had Jugge's mark (no. 151).[24]

Christopher Barker, who was granted a license in 1575,[25] then became "Printer to the Queens Majesty." Along with his publication of Geneva Bibles, Barker also issued a folio of the Bishops' in 1578 (no. 155), a folio (no. 185) and a quarto in 1584 (no. 186), a folio in 1585 that had the Bishops' Psalms (no. 188), a folio in 1588 (no. 198), and a folio in 1591 (no. 155). Christopher Barker died November 29, 1599. The last edition of the Bishops' Bible (1602; no. 171) was by Robert Barker. Earlier bibliographers projected an edition of the Bishops Bible in 1606. This claim is now rejected.[26]

The *Historical Catalogue* lists two previously unidentified Bishops' New Testaments by Jugge in 1568 (nos. 123, 124). The text printed in black letter is not divided into verses; the arguments and headings are in Roman letter. Dore lists issues of the Bishops' New Testament, not included in the *Historical Catalogue*, in 1570 in a quarto and in a smaller size. There were quartos in 1575 and 1576. A 1577 Testament in black letter type did not have the text divided into verses.[27] An unknown printer (probably Barker) issued a Testament in 1578 (no. 157). Another was in 1579 (no. 163). Christopher Barker issued a printing in 1581 (no. 172) and another in 1582 (no. 176).

---

24. Numbers here and later are those of Herbert, *Historical Catalogue*.
25. Butterworth, *Literary Lineage of the King James Bible*, 187.
26. See Herbert, *Historical Catalogue*, no. 1502.
27. Dore, *Old Bibles*, 275.

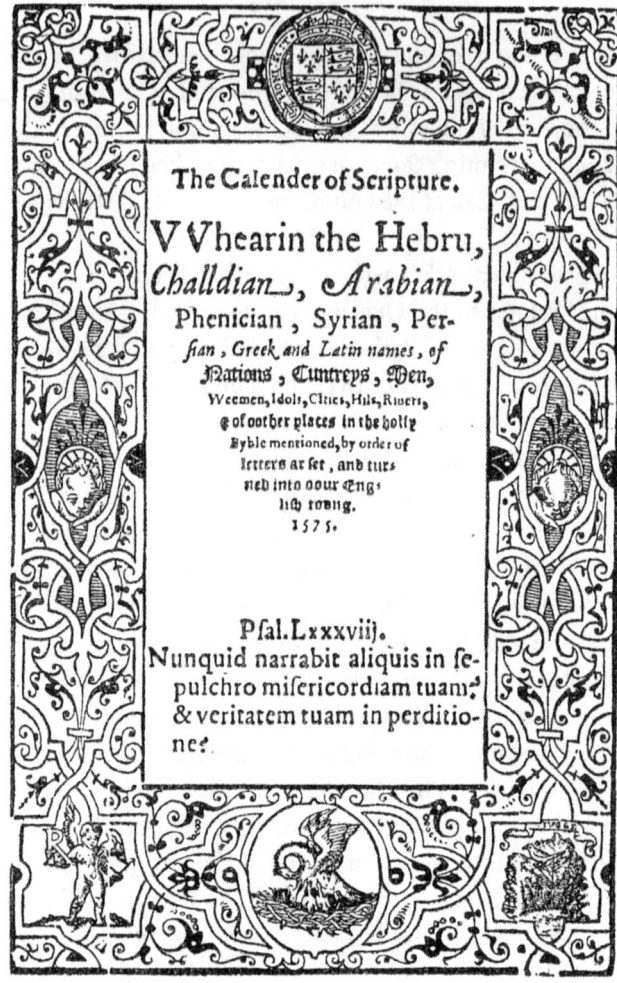

Figure 36: Woodcut border with pelican feeding her young, printer's device of Richard Jugge, at center bottom, at lower right nightingale in thorn bush with "ivgge" above (1575).

Conclusion

Figure 37: Title to New Testament in Christopher Barker's 1583 Bible, Tetragrammaton at top between two cherubs, "ER" at either side, "C.B." within center opening.

In 1589, the Bishops' and the Rheims New Testament were printed side by side in a work by William Fulke, who sought to refute accusations made by the Catholics (no. 202). The work went through several editions (1601 [no. 265], 1617 [nos. 359, 360], 1633 [no. 480]) giving the Rheims New Testament wider circulation than it otherwise would have had. The Bishops' is identified as "The Translation of the Church of England."

Meanwhile, printings of the Bishops' New Testament continued. A 1595 (no. 228) edition is for the deputies of Barker, as is a 1596 (no. 232), a 1597 (no. 241), a 1598 (no. 245), and a 1600 (no. 259). A 1605 octavo was by the deputy of Barker (nos. 282, 283, 284). A 1606 octavo was a 1613 edition (no. 328) preceded by the Great Bible Psalms, a 1614 (no. 327), a 1615 (no. 344), and a 1617 (nos. 356, 357, 358).

In the Churches

An account book of Saint John's College, Cambridge, has the entry for 1571, "For a new Bible in English, the last translation, 27s 8d."[28] At the time of its issuing, the Bishops' Bible was in competition with the Great Bible, which enjoyed eight editions during Elizabeth's reign (nos. 110, 117, 119, 120, 122, 127, 128, and 129)[29] with the last printing in 1569. Copies, however, could have long remained in the churches. Tyndale's New Testament saw additional printings in 1561 and 1566 (nos. 111, 112, 113, 114, 115, and 121). Most of the visitation articles merely require a Bible of the largest size.

The Bishops' was also in competition with the more popular Geneva Bible, which until 1575 was printed abroad only and not in England. Eadie estimated that across the career of Elizabeth there were three printings of the Geneva for each one printing of the Bishops'.[30] Archbishop Grindel, who succeeded Parker in 1575, favored the Geneva. Late in Elizabeth's reign (1582), the Rheims

---

28. Herbert, *Historical Catalogue*, no. 70.
29. Mombert, *English Versions of the Bible*, 168.
30. Eadie, *English Bible*, 2:102.

Conclusion

New Testament also entered the picture; the Douay Old Testament was prepared but for lack of resources was not issued until 1610. Elizabeth neither fostered nor hindered the free printings and circulation of these various versions. John Whitgift became archbishop of Canterbury in 1583 and ordered Barker to resume publication of the Bishops' Bible. Two printings are thought to be the outcome. Whitgift did not hinder sale of the Geneva Bible.

About a table of genealogy before the New Testament in the 1585 folio edition, Hugh Broughton remarked of the errors, "Our Bishops' Bible might well give place too the Alkoran, pestered with lyes."[31] The Psalms of this edition are those of the Bishops' revision. Peter Levi has published selected reprinted samples of Broughton's Bible translation.[32] The Spanish Armada was demolished November 19, 1588, and Elizabeth no longer need fear interventions from the continent.

It has been convincingly argued that William Shakespeare in his earlier plays reflects a knowledge of the Bishops' Bible though his later plays reflect the Geneva Bible.[33]

Rule one, directing the King James translators, stated that the Bishops' Bible was to be followed and altered as little "as the Truth of the original will permit."[34] Robert Barker, the printer, supplied forty unbound copies of the 1602 Bishops' Bible for use of the translating committees.[35] Only one survives. A 1602 edition of the Bishops' in the Bodlian Library has written notes in the margins assumed to be those made in preparing the King James Version.[36] Cotton conjectures that the Bodleian Library Bible had "MS corrections for the new translation designed by king James."[37] Westcott, on the other hand, rejected this case and insisted that

---

31. *STC*, 3844, 47.
32. Levi, *English Bible*, 176–91.
33. Noble, *Shakespeare's Biblical Knowledge*, 69–76.
34. Pollard, *Records of the English Bible*, 53.
35. Norton, *Textual History of the King James Bible*, 12.
36. Jacobs, "Bodlian Bishops' Bible"; Bois, *Translating for King James*; Allen and Jacobs, *King James Gospels*.
37. Cotton, *Editions of the Bible*, 56, note.

the notes were merely those of a scholar's collation of the Royal and Bishops' texts with an attempt to trace the corrections.[38] More recently, Willoughby has reopened this question and set forth the hypothesis that this Bible as well as the Lambeth Palace maps are preliminary stages in the process, but not the last revisions.[39]

John Selden, a member of one of the committees, described committee procedure: "they met together, and one read the Translation, the rest holding in their Hands some Bible, either of the learned Tongues, or *French, Spanish, Italian*, etc. if they found any Fault, they spoke, if not, he read on."[40] The Bible the reader would have used would have been a Bishops'. Selden was more complimentary of the Bishops' than the reviewers of the nineteenth and twentieth centuries: "The *English* Translation of the Bible is the best Translation in the World, and renders the Sense of the Original best, taking in for the *English* Translation, the Bishops' Bible as well as King *James*".[41]

Butterworth estimated that 4 percent of the English wording of the King James Bible is owed to Wycliffe, 18 percent to Tyndale, 13 percent to Coverdale, 19 percent to the Geneva Bible, but 39 percent to the King James Version revisers.[42] David Norton argues that changes from the 1611 edition in the several following editions show restoration of 1602 Bishops' readings.[43]

Readers of the King James Version find "persecuted for righteousness' sake" (Matt 5:10), "faithless and perverse generation" (Matt 17:17), and "overcome evil with good" (Rom 12:21). Numerous other examples are listed by Samuel McComb.[44]

P. Marion Simms projected that the Bishops' Bible may have been used in California on American shores by the chaplain of Sir Francis Drake in 1579 and by Sir Humphrey Gilbert

38. Westcott, *General View of the History*, 156–57, note.
39. Willoughby, *Making of the King James Bible*, 71–72.
40. Selden, *Table-Talk*, 6.
41. Ibid., 5.
42. Butterworth, *Literary Lineage of the King James Bible*, 231, 237.
43. Norton, *Textual History of the King James Bible*, 41.
44. McComb, *Making of the English Bible*, 59–61.

Conclusion

in Newfoundland in 1583. Sir Walter Raleigh's colony in North Carolina had a Bible. Thomas Heriot in 1585 had a Bible at Roanoke Island. The reasoning is that these colonies did not represent Puritans who would have favored the Geneva Bible. The same is true of George Popham's settlement in Maine at the mouth of the Kennebec River in 1607. The colony had Richard Seymer as its preacher. The evidence is only circumstantial. The sources do not specify the version in any of these cases. There had been ample editions of the Bishops' in quarto transportable size.[45]

A copy of the Bishops' Bible in the Folger Shakespeare Library of Washington, DC, has family records entered in the nineteenth century.

The *English Hexapla* by Samuel Bagster in 1841 (no. 1840) had a New Testament text for Wycliff, Tyndale, Cranmer, Genevan, Anglo-Rheimes, and Authorized Versions, but did not include the Bishops'. Jacob I. Mombert printed selected sections of the Bishops' text.[46] *The New Testament Octapla* by Luther A. Weigle printed the 1602 text (but not the notes),[47] and *The Genesis Octapla* did the same for the book of Genesis.[48] Selected Bishops' sections without notes are printed by Peter Levi.[49]

An unsympathetic review of this Bible was done by Nicholas Pocock.[50] Granting all the shortcomings eighteenth to twenty-first century-scholarship can find in the Bishops' Bible, it was an important stage in moving English people from prohibited Bible reading to being a Bible-reading people. The revisers labored to give God's book to God's people in a language they could understand. The King James translators did not think they were making a bad translation into a good one, but were making a good one better.[51]

45. Simms, *Bible in America*, 72–82.
46. Mombert, *English Versions of the Bible*, 280–90.
47. Weigle, *New Testament Octapla*.
48. Weigle, *Genesis Octapla*.
49. Levi, *English Bible*, 110–26.
50. Pocock, "Bishops' Bible," 33–37, 67–71, 111–16, 148–49; ibid., "Bishops' Bible of 1568," 243–45.
51. Rhodes and Lupas, *Translators to the Reader*, 81.

Appendix

Editions of the Bishop's Bible

STC	DM	Brief Title and Date
2099	89	The holie bible 5 pts. fol. R. Jugge, [1568]
2105	93	The holi bible 5 pts. 4o R. Jugge, 1569
2107	96	The holie bible 5 pts. fol. R. Jugge, 1572
2108	100	The holie byble 5 pts. 4o R. Jugge, 1573
2109	101	The holy byble 5 pts. fol. R. Jugge, 1574 (July 5)
2110	103	The holy byble 5 pts. fol. W. Norton, 1575 (Nov 24)
2111	103	[Variant, reading in imprint:] L. Harison
2112	103	[Variant, in imprint:] F. Coldock
2113	103	[Variant, in imprint:] G. Dewes
2113a	103	[Variant, in imprint:] J. Walley
2114	104	The holy byble 5 pts. 4o R. Jugge, 1575
2115	108	The holy byble 5 pts. 4o R. Jugge, 1576
2121	112	The holy byble 4o R. Jugge, 1577
2122	113	[Anr. ed.] sm. 4o R. Jugge, 1577

APPENDIX

STC	DM	Brief Title and Date
2124	116	The holy byble 5 pts. fol. by the Assignement of C. Barker, 1578
2141	141	The holy bible fol. C. Barker, 1584
2142	142	[Anr. ed.] 4o C. Barker, 1584
2143	144	[Anr. ed.] fol. C. Barker, 1585
2149	152	The holy bible fol. Deputies of C. Barker, 1588
2156	160	The holy bible fol. Deputies of C. Barker, 1591
2167	175	The holy bible fol. Deputies of C. Barker, 1595
2188	206	The holy bible fol. R. Barker, 1602
2874	97	[Anr. ed. Bps. version of 1572] 4o R. Watkins, [1573–75?]
2875	98	[Anr. ed.] 8o R. Jugge, [1573–75?]
2875a	99	[Anr. ed. or variant] 4o [R. Jugge? 1573–75?]
		The Newe Testament 8o C. Barker, 1579
2883	133	The newe test. 8o C. Barker, 1582
2888	156	The text of the new test. W. Fulke. fol. Deputies of C. Barker, 1589
2893	176	The new test. 8o the Deputy of C. Barker, 1595
2896	186	[The new test.] 8o Deputy of C. Barker, 1598
2897	196	The new test. 8o Deputy of C. Barker, 1600
2900	202	The text of the new test. W. Fulke. fol. R. Barker, 1601
		The text of the new test. W. Fulke. fol. but imprint: Londini, Impensis G. B., 1601
2904	216	The new test. 8o Deputy of R. Barker, 1605
	217	[Anr. ed.] date unknown

Appendix

STC	DM	Brief Title and Date
	218	[Anr. ed.] date unknown
2905	221	[Anr. ed.] 8o R. Barker, 1606
2906	229	[Anr. ed.] 8o R. Barker, 1608
2912	254	The new test. 8o R. Barker, 1613
2914	268	[The new test.] 8o R. Barker, 1615
2916	275	The new test. 8o R. Barker, 1617
2917	278	The text of the new test. W. Fulke. fol. T. Adams, 1617
2918	275	[Anr. issue with imprint:] J. Bill, 1617
2947	371	The text of the new test. W. Fulke, 4th ed. fol. A. Matthewes, 1633
2961	95	The gospels of the fower euangelistes. 4o J. Daye, 1571

Bibliography

Allen, Ward S., and Edward C. Jacobs. *The Coming of the King James Gospels: A Collation of the Translators' Work-in-Progress*. Fayetteville, AR: University of Arkansas Press, 1995.

Ames, Joseph. *Typographical Antiquities: Or the History of Printing in England, Scotland, and Ireland*. Edited by Thomas Frognall Dibdin. 4 vols. London: Longman, et al., 1819.

Anderson, Christopher. *The Annals of the English Bible*. London: Jackson, Walford, & Hodder, 1862.

Arber, Edward, ed. *A Transcript of the Registers of the Company of Stationers of London, 1554–1640 A.D.* 5 vols. London: Privately printed, 1875–77.

Aston, Margaret. "The *Bishops' Bible* Illustrations." In *The Church and the Arts: Papers Read at the 1990 Summer Meeting and the 1991 Winter Meeting of the Ecclesiastical History Society*, edited by Diana Wood, 267–85. Studies in Church History 28. Oxford: Blackwell, 1992.

Ayre, John, ed. *The Early Works of Thomas Becon, Being the Treatises Published by Him in the Reign of King Henry VIII*. The Parker Society. Cambridge: University Press, 1843.

Bacon, Francis. *The Moral and Historical Works of Lord Bacon*. London: Bohn, 1852.

Barlow, William. *The Summe and Substance of the Conference Which it Pleased His Excellent Majestie to Have with the Lords, Bishops, and Other of His Clergie at Hampton Court, January 14, 1603 (1604)*. London: Windet, 1604.

Beloe, William. *Anecdotes of Literature and Scarce Books*. 6 vols. London: Rivington, 1807–12.

Beresford, J. R. "The Churchwardens, Accounts of Holy Trinity, Chester, 1532–1633." *Journal of the Chester and North Wales Archaeological, Architectural and Historical Society* n.s. 38 (1951) 95–172.

Blades, William. *Books in Chains and Other Biographical Papers*. London: Stock, 1892.

Bois, John. *Translating for King James*. Translated and edited by Allen Ward. Nashville: Vanderbilt University Press, 1969.

Bibliography

Brayley, Edward Wedlake. *A Topographical History of Surrey*. 5 vols. London: Willis, 1840.

Broughton, Hugh. *A Censure of the Late Translation for Our Churches*. Middleburg: Schilders, 1612.

Brown, Alexander. *The Genesis of the United States: A Narrative of the Movement in England, 1605–1616*. 2 vols. Boston: Houghton Mifflin, 1890.

Bruce, John, and Thomas Thomason Perowne, eds. *Correspondence of Matthew Parker . . . Comprising Letters Written by and to Him, from A.D. 1535, to His Death, A.D. 1575*. The Parker Society Publications 33. Cambridge: University Press, 1853.

Bruton, John R. *A History of Bewdley with Concise Accounts of Some Neighboring Parishes*. London: Reeves, 1883.

Burleson, Hugh L., ed. *How Our Church Came to Our Country*. Milwaukee, WI: Morehouse, 1920.

Burrage, Henry S. *The Beginnings of Colonial Maine: 1602–1658*. Portland, ME: Marks, 1914.

Butterworth, Charles C. *The Literary Lineage of the King James Bible, 1340–1611*. Philadelphia: University of Pennsylvania Press, 1941.

Cardwell, Edward. *Synodalia: A Collection of Articles of Religion, Canons, and Proceedings of Convocations in the Province of Canterbury, from the Year 1547 to the Year 1717*. 2 vols. Oxford: University Press, 1842.

Chandler, Charles. *Notes on the Parish of Redenhall with Harlestone*. London: Jerrold, 1896.

Clair, Colin. "The Bishops' Bible 1568." *Gutenberg Jahrbuch* (1962) 287–90.

———. *A History of Printing in Britain*. London: Cassell, 1965.

Cooper, Charles Henry, and Thompson Cooper. *Athenae Cantabrigienses*. 2 vols. Cambridge: Macmillan, 1858.

Corbett, Margery, and Michael Norton. *Engraving in England in the Sixteenth and Seventeenth Centuries: A Descriptive Catalogue with Introductions*. Cambridge: University Press, 1964.

Cornish, Robert, ed. *Kilmington Churchwardens' Accounts*. Exeter, ENG: W. Pollard, 1901.

Cotton, Henry. *Editions of the Bible and Parts Thereof in English, from the Year MDV to MDCCCL*. 2nd ed. Oxford: University Press, 1852.

Cox, John Charles, ed. *Churchwardens' Accounts from the Fourteenth Century to the Close of the Seventeenth Century*. London: Metheun, 1913.

Darlow, Thomas Herbert, and Horace Frederick Moule. *Historical Catalogue of the Printed Editions of Holy Scripture in the Library of the British and Foreign Bible Society*. 2 vols. New York: Kraus, 1963.

Davidson, Randall T. "The Authorisation of the English Bible." *Macmillan's Magazine* 44 (1881) 436–44.

Davies, James. *A Relation of a Voyage to Sagadahoc*. Edited by B. F. Decosta. Cambridge: University Press, 1880.

Dictionary of American Biography. Edited by Allen Johnson et al. 20 vols. New York: Scribner's, 1928–37.

Bibliography

Dictionary of National Biography. Edited by Leslie Stephen and Sidney Lee. 22 vols. London: Oxford University Press, 1921-22.

Dore, John Read. *Old Bibles: An Account of the Early Versions of the English Bible.* 2nd ed. London: Eyre & Spottiswoode, 1888.

Drew, Charles, ed. *Lambeth Churchwardens' Accounts, 1504-1645.* Surrey Record Society. London: Butler & Tanner, 1940.

Eadie, John. *The English Bible: An External and Critical History of the Various English Translations of Scripture.* 2 vols. London: Macmillan, 1876.

Edgar, Andrew. *The Bibles of England: A Plain Account for Plain People of the Principal Versions of the Bible in English.* London: Gardner, 1889.

Fallow, T. M., ed. "Some Elizabethan Visitations of the Churches Belonging to the Peculiar of the Dean of York." *Yorkshire Archaeological Journal* 18 (1905) 197-232, 313-40.

Farmiloe, James Ernest, and Rosita Nixseaman, eds. *Elizabethan Churchwardens' Accounts.* Publications of the Bedfordshire Historical Record Society 33. Streatley, ENG: Bedfordshire Historical Record Society, 1953.

Fincham, Kenneth, ed. *Visitation Articles and Injunctions of the Early Stuart Church.* 2 vols. Church of England Record Society 1 & 5. London: Boydell & Brewer, 1994, 1998.

Foster, Charles Wilmer, ed. *Lincoln Episcopal Records in the Time of Thomas Cooper, 1571-1584.* Publications of the Lincoln Record Society 2. London: Lincoln Record Society, 1912.

Foster, John Ebenezer, ed. *Churchwardens' Accounts of St. Mary the Great, Cambridge, 1504-1635.* Cambridge: Antiquarian Society, 1950.

Foxe, John. *The Acts and Monuments of the Church: Containing the History and Sufferings of the Martyrs.* Edited by Michael Hobart Seymour. London: Scott, Webster & Geary, 1838.

Frere, Walter Howard, and Charles Edward Douglas, eds. *Puritan Manifestoes: A Study of the Origin of the Puritan Revolt.* London: SPCK, 1954.

Fuller, Thomas. *The Church History of Britain: From the Birth of Jesus Christ until the Year 1648.* 6 vols. Oxford: University Press, 1845.

———. *The History of the Worthies of England.* 3 vols. Edited by P. Austin Nuttall. London: Tegg, 1840.

Gairdner, James. *The English Church in the Sixteenth Century, from the Accession of Henry VIII to the Death of Mary.* London: Macmillan, 1902.

Garrett, Christina Hallowell. *The Marian Exiles: A Study in the Origins of Elizabethan Puritanism.* Cambridge: University Press, 1938.

Garry, Francis N. A., and A. G. Garry. *The Churchwardens' Accounts of the Parish of Saint Mary's, Reading, Berks, 1550-1662.* Reading, ENG: Blackwell, 1893.

Gee, Henry, and William John Hardy. *Documents Illustrative of English Church History.* London: Macmillan, 1910.

Ginsburg, Christian D. "Shakespeare's Use of the Bible." *Athenaeum* 2896 (April 1883) 541-42.

Bibliography

Glasscock, Joseph L., ed. *The Records of St. Michael's Parish Church, Bishop Stortford*. London: Stock, 1881.

Greenslade, Stanley Lawrence, ed. *The West from the Reformation to the Present Day*. Vol. 3, *The Cambridge History of the Bible*. Edited by Peter R. Ackroyd et al. 3 vols. Cambridge: University Press, 1963.

Haines, Walter. "Stanford Churchwardens' Accounts 1552–1602." *Antiquary* 17 (1888) 168–72.

Hakluyt, Richard. *The Principal Navigations, Voyages, Traffiques and Discoveries of the English Nation*. Edited by Edmund Goldsmid. 12 vols. London: Bishop, Newberie & Barker, 1598–1600.

Harington, John. *Nugae Antiquae: Being a Miscellaneous Collection of Original Papers, in Prose and Verse*. 2 vols. London: Vernor et al., 1804.

HarperCollins Bible Dictionary. Edited by Paul J. Achtemeier et al. Rev. ed. New York: HarperCollins, 1996.

Hartshorne, Charles Henry. *The Book Rarities in the University of Cambridge*. London: Longman, 1829.

Heaton, William James. *The Puritan Bible and Other Contemporaneous Protestant Versions*. London: Griffiths, 1913.

Herbert, Arthur Sumner. *Historical Catalogue of Printed Editions of the English Bible: 1525–1961*. London: British & Foreign Bible Society, 1968.

Hind, Arthur M. *Engraving in England in the Sixteenth and Seventeenth Centuries*. 3 vols. Cambridge: University Press, 1952–64.

Hobhouse, Edmund, ed. *Churchwardens' Accounts of Croscombe, Pilton, Yatton, Tintinhull, Morebath and St. Michael, Bath, Ranging from A.D. 1349 to 1560*. Somerset Record Society 4. London: Harrison, 1890.

Holland, William. *Cratfield: A Transcript of the Accounts of the Parish from A.D. 1490 to A.D. 1642*. London: Jarrold & Sons, 1885.

Hotchkiss, Valerie R., and Charles Caldwell Ryrie, eds. *Formatting the Word of God the Charles Caldwell Ryrie Collection: An Exhibition at Bridwell Library, Perkins School of Theology, Southern Methodist University, October 1998 through January 1999*. Dallas, TX: Bridwell Library, 1998.

Hughes, J. E., ed. "Cheswardine Churchwardens' Account Book, 1544–1628." In *Shropshire Parish Documents*, edited by E. C. Peele and R. S. Clease, 52–79. Shrewsbury, ENG: W. B. Walker, 1920.

Hussey, Arthur. "Visitations of the Archdeacon of Canterbury." *Archaeologia Cantiana* 25 (1902) 11–56; 26 (1904) 17–50; 27 (1905) 213–29.

The Injunctions and Other Ecclesiastical Proceedings of Richard Barnes, Bishop of Durham, from 1575–1587. Publications of the Surtees Society 22. London: Bentley, 1750.

Irvine, Nicholas Ferguson. "Visitation of Warrington Deanery by the Bishop of Chester in the Year 1592." *Lancashire and Cheshire Historical Society Transactions* n.s. 10 (1895) 183–92.

Jacobs, Edward Craney. "A Bodleian Bishops' Bible, 1602 (Bib. Eng. 1601 b. 1): A Preliminary Study of the Old Testament Annotations and Their

Relationship to the Authorized Version, 1611." PhD diss., Auburn University, 1972.
Jenkins, Claude, ed. *Act Book of the Archdeacon of Taunton, 1623*. Somerset Record Society 43. London: Somerset Record Society, 1928.
Johnson, Alfred Forbes. *A Catalogue of Engraved and Etched English Title-Pages Down to the Death of William Faithorne, 1691*. Bibliographical Society Facsimiles and Illustrations 4. Oxford: University Press, 1933.
Kennedy, William Paul McClure. *Elizabethan Episcopal Administration: An Essay in Sociology and Politics*. London: Mowbray, 1924.
Kenyon, Frederick George. *Our Bible and the Ancient Manuscripts: Being a History of the Text and Its Translations*. 4th ed. London: Eyre & Spottiswoode, 1903.
Kitto, John Vivian, ed. *Saint Martin-in-the-Fields: The Accounts of the Church Wardens, 1525-1603*. London: Simpkin & Marshall, 1901.
Knappen, Marshall Mason. *Tudor Puritanism: A Chapter in the History of Idealism*. Gloucester, MA: P. Smith, 1963 [c.1939].
Levi, Peter. *The English Bible, 1534-1850*. Grand Rapids: Eerdmans, 1974.
Lewis, Jack P. *The English Bible from KJV to NIV: A History and Evaluation*. Grand Rapids: Baker, 1981.
———. *Questions You've Asked about Bible Translations*. Searcy, AR: Resource Publications, 1991.
Lewis, John. *A Complete History of the Several Translations of the Holy Bible and New Testament into English*. 3rd ed. London: Baynes, 1818.
Lovett, Richard. *The English Bible in the John Rylands Library, 1525 to 1640*. Manchester: John Rylands Library, 1899.
Lucas, Henry Stephen. *The Renaissance and the Reformation*. 2nd ed. New York: Harper, 1960.
Lupton, Lewis Frederick. *A History of the Geneva Bible*. 22 vols. London: Fauconbert, 1966-90.
MacRay, William Dunn. *Annals of the Bodleian Library, Oxford*. 2nd ed. Oxford: Clarendon, 1890.
McComb, Samuel. *The Making of the English Bible*. New York: Yard, 1909.
McKerrow, Ronald Brunlees, and Frederic Sutherland Ferguson. *Title-Page Borders Used in England and Scotland, 1435-1640*. Oxford: University Press, 1931.
Mellows, William Thomas. *Peterborough Local Administration: Parochial Government before the Reformation*. Peterborough, ENG: Northampton Record Society, 1939.
Mombert, Jacob Isidor. *English Versions of the Bible: A Hand-book with Copious Examples Illustrating the Ancestry and Relationship of the Several Versions, and Comparative Tables*. London: Bagster, 1906.
Moulton, William Fiddian. *The History of the English Bible*. London: Kelly, 1911.
Mozley, James Frederic. *Coverdale and His Bibles*. London: Lutterworth, 1953.
Nevinson, Charles, ed. *Later Writings of Bishop Hooper, Together with His Letters and Other Pieces*. The Parker Society. Cambridge: University Press, 1852.

Bibliography

Newcome, Richard. *A Memoir of Gabriel Goodman, D.D.* Ruthin, WAL: Taliesin, 1825.

Nichols, John. *Illustrations of the Manners and Expenses of Ancient Times in England in Centuries XVI–XVII.* London: Society of Antiquaries, 1797.

Nicholson, William, ed. *The Remains of Edmund Grindal: Successively Bishop of London and Archbishop of York and Canterbury.* The Parker Society. Cambridge: University Press, 1843.

Noble, Richmond Samuel Howe. *Shakespeare's Biblical Knowledge and Use of the Book of Common Prayer.* New York: Octagon, 1970.

North, Thomas, ed. *The Accounts of the Church Wardens of St. Martins, Leicester, 1489–1844.* Leicester, ENG: Clarke, 1884.

Norton, David. *A Textual History of the King James Bible.* Cambridge: University Press, 2005.

Overall, William Henry, ed. *The Accounts of the Churchwardens of the Parish of St. Michael, Cornhill in the City of London from 1456–1608.* London: Waterlow, 1871.

Peel, Albert, ed. *The Seconde Parte of a Register: Being a Calendar of Manuscripts under That Title Intended for Publication by the Puritans about 1593.* 2 vols. Cambridge: University Press, 1915.

Perry, William Stevens. *The Connection of the Church of England with Early American Discovery and Colonization.* Portland, ME: s.n., 1863.

———. *The History of the American Episcopal Church, 1587–1883.* 2 vols. Boston: Osgood, 1885.

Pettigrew, Thomas Joseph. *Bibliotheca Sussexiana: A Descriptive Catalogue.* 2 vols. London: Longman, 1839.

Peyton, Sidney A., ed. *The Churchwardens' Presentments in the Oxfordshire Peculiars of Dorchester, Thame, and Banbury.* Oxfordshire Record Society Series 10. Dorchester: Oxfordshire Record Society, 1928.

Phillimore, Robert. *The Ecclesiastical Law of the Church of England.* 2 vols. London: Sweet, 1873.

Plomer, Henry Robert, ed. *The Churchwardens' Accounts of St. Nicholas, Strood.* Kent Archaeological Society Records 5. Ashford, ENG: Kent Records, 1927.

Pocock, Nicholas. "The Bishops' Bible." *Bibliographer* 1 (January 1882) 33–37, 67–71, 111–16, 148–49.

———. "The Bishops' Bible of 1568, 1572, and 1602." *Athenaeum* 25 (February 1888) 243–45.

Pollard, Alfred William. "Peerson or Pierson, Andrew." In *DNB* 15:677.

———, ed. *Records of the English Bible: The Documents Relating to the Translation and Publication of the Bible in English, 1525–1611.* London: Oxford University Press, 1911.

Pollard, Alfred William, and Gilbert Richard Redgrave. *A Short-Title Catalogue of Books Printed in England, Scotland, and Ireland and of English Books Printed Abroad, 1475–1640.* London: Bibliographical Society, 1963 [1926].

Bibliography

Povah, Alred. *The Annals of the Parishes of St. Olave Hart Street and All Hallows, Staining, in the City of London*. London: Blades, East & Blades, 1824.

Price, Ira Maurice. *The Ancestry of Our English Bible: An Account of Manuscripts, Texts, and Versions of the Bible*. New York: Harper, 1949.

Purchas, Samuel. *Hakluytus Posthumus or Purchas His Pilgrims*. 4 vols. London: Stansby, 1625.

Purvis, John Stanley. *Tudor Parish Documents of the Diocese of York*. Cambridge: University Press, 1949.

Remains Historical and Literary Connected with the Palatine Counties of Lancaster and Chester. Manchester: Chetham Society, 1885.

Rhodes, Erroll Franklin, and Liana Lupas, eds. *The Translators to the Reader: The Original Preface of the King James Version of 1611 Revisited*. New York: American Bible Society, 1997.

Robinson, Hastings, trans. and ed. *The Zurich Letters: Comprising the Correspondence of Several English Bishops and Others*. The Parker Society. Cambridge: University Press, 1842.

Savage, Richard, ed. *The Churchwardens' Accounts of the Parish of St. Nicholas, Warwickshire 1547–1621*. Warwick, ENG: Cooke, 1890.

Sayle, Charles Edward. *Early English Printed Books in the University Library, Cambridge, 1475 to 1640*. 4 vols. Cambridge: University Press, 1900.

Selden, John. *Table-Talk*. Edited by Edward Arber. London: Murray, 1868.

Shea, John Gilmary. "The Bible in American History." *American Catholic Quarterly Review* 3 (1878) 131–35.

Simms, P. Marian. *The Bible in America*. New York: Erickson, 1936.

Skaife, Robert H. "Extracts from the Visitation Books at York." *Yorkshire Archaeological Journal* 15 (1900) 224–43.

Somers, John. *Somers Tracts: A Collection of Scarce and Valuable Tracts on the Most Interesting and Entertaining Subjects*. 7 vols. London: Cadell & Davies, 1809.

Smith, John. *Generall Historie of Virginia, New England, etc*. London: I. D. & I. H. for Michael Sparks, 1624.

Smith, John Edward. *A Catalogue of Westminster Records Deposited at the Town Hall, in the Custody of the Vestry of St. Margaret and St. John*. London: Wightman, 1900.

Strachey, William. *The Historie of Travell into Virginia Britania*. Edited by L. B. Wright and Virginia Fruend. London: Printed for the Hakluyt Society, 1953.

Streeter, Burnett Hilman. *The Chained Library: A Survey of Four Centuries in the Evolution of the English Library*. London: Macmillan, 1931.

Strype, John. *The History of the Life and Acts of the Most Reverend Father in God, Edmund Grindal*. London: Hartley, 1710.

———. *The Life and Acts of John Whitgift, D.D., the Third and Last Archbishop of Canterbury in the Reign of Queen Elizabeth*. 3 vols. Oxford: Clarendon, 1822.

Bibliography

———. *The Life and Acts of Matthew Parker the First Archbishop of Canterbury.* 3 vols. Oxford: Clarendon, 1821.

———. *Memorials of the Most Reverend Father in God, Thomas Cranmer.* 2 vols. London: Routledge, 1853.

Swayne, Henry James Fowle, ed. *Churchwardens' Accounts of S. Edmund & S. Thomas, Sarum, 1443–1702, with Other Documents.* Salisbury, ENG: Bennett, 1896.

Tanner, Thomas. *Bibliotheca Britannico-Hibernica.* London: G. Bowyer, 1748.

Thomas, David Richard. *The Life and Work of Bishop Davies and William Salesbury.* Oswestry, ENG: Caxton, 1902.

Ward, Thomas. *England's Reformation: A Poem in Four Cantos.* New York: Sadlier, 1845.

Watney, Thomas. *Some Account of the Hospital of St. Thomas of Acorn in the Cheap, London, and of the Plate of the Mercers' Company.* London: Blades, East & Blades, 1906.

Watt, Robert. *Bibliotheca Britannica or a General Index of British and Foreign Literature.* 4 vols. Edinburgh: Constable, 1824.

Webster's New Biographical Dictionary. Springfield, MA: Merriam-Webster, 1995.

Weddall, George Edward. "Churchwardens' Accounts and Other Documents Relating to Howden." *Yorkshire Archaeological Journal* 19 (1907) 455–81.

Weigle, Luther Allan. *The Genesis Octapla: Eight English Versions of the Book of Genesis in the Tyndale-King James Tradition.* London: Nelson, 1965.

———. *The New Testament Octapla: Eight English Versions of the New Testament in the Tyndale-King James Tradition.* Edinburgh: Nelson, 1962.

Westcott, Brooke Foss. *A General View of the History of the English Bible.* 3rd ed. Revised by William Aldis Wright. London: Macmillan, 1905.

White, Francis Overend. *Lives of the Elizabethan Bishops of the Anglican Church.* London: Skeffington, 1898.

Williams, John Foster, ed. *Diocese of Norwich, Bishop Redman's Visitation, 1597.* Publications of the Norfolk Record Society 18. Norfolk, ENG: Norfolk Record Society, 1946.

Willoughby, Edwin Eliott. *The Making of the King James Bible.* Los Angeles: Plantin, 1956.

Wing, Donald Goddard. *Short-Title Catalogue of Books Printed in England, Scotland, Ireland, Wales, and British America and of English Books Printed in Other Countries, 1641–1700.* 3 vols. New York: Index Society, 1945–51.

Wingfield, Edward Maria. *A Discourse on Virginia.* Edited by Charles Deane. Boston: American Antiquarian Society, 1860.

Wood, Anthony à. *Athenae Oxonienses: An Exact History of All the Writers and Bishops Who Have Had Their Education in the University of Oxford.* 2 vols. London: Rivington, 1813.

Wright, Thomas, ed. *Churchwardens' Accounts for the Town of Ludlow in Shropshire, from 1540 to the End of the Reign of Queen Elizabeth.* Westminster: Camden Society, 1869.

www.ingramcontent.com/pod-product-compliance
Lightning Source LLC
Chambersburg PA
CBHW051937160426
43198CB00013B/2186